AINSLEY HARRIOTT

my favourite hot and spicy recipes

This paperback edition first published in Australia and New Zealand by
BBC Worldwide Ltd in 2003.

BBC Worldwide Ltd,
Woodlands, 80 Wood Lane,
London W12 0TT

The recipes contained in this book first appeared in *In the Kitchen with Ainsley
Harriott*, which was originally published by BBC Worldwide in 1996 (photographs
by Philip Webb), *Ainsley Harriott's Barbecue Bible*, which was originally published by
BBC Worldwide in 1997 (photographs by Gus Filgate), *Ainsley Harriott's Meals in
Minutes*, which was originally published by BBC Worldwide in 1998 (photographs by
Juliet Piddington and Roger Stowell), and *Ainsley's Big Cook Out*, which was originally
published by BBC Worldwide in 1999 (photographs by Gus Filgate).

ISBN 0 563 48728 3

Commissioning Editor: Rachel Copus
Project Editor: Julia Zimmermann
Design Manager: Sarah Ponder
Designer: Kathryn Gammon
Typographic Styling: Paul Welti
Recipes developed and written in association with Silvana Franco, Debbie Major,
Vicky Musselman and Angela Nilsen
Home Economists: Lorna Brash, Maxine Clarke, Silvana Franco, Vicky Musselman,
Angela Nilsen, Sarah Ramsbottom
Production Controller: Kenneth McKay
Author Photograph: Craig Easton

Set in Helvetica Neue
Printed and bound in Great Britain by Butler and Tanner Ltd, Frome and London
Colour reproduction by Radstock Reproductions Ltd, Midsomer Norton

Front cover photograph by Gus Filgate: *Aubergine Stuffed with Asian Vegetables*
(page 110)

AINSLEY HARRIOTT

my favourite hot and spicy recipes

contents

introduction

Ever since I first learned to cook in my mum's kitchen at home, I've been fascinated by unfamiliar flavours and have always enjoyed experimenting with new and unusual ingredients in my cooking. One of the things that I love about being a TV chef is being able to pass that enthusiasm on to other people, which is why I was so delighted when the BBC asked me to choose my 100 favourite hot and spicy recipes to share with you in this book.

Over recent years I've noticed that we have all become much more adventurous about the kinds of food we are eating. I have found this outlook particularly true amongst Australians and New Zealanders on my recent trips there. With an ever-increasing number of people travelling to far-flung corners of the globe, attitudes towards food are changing. People are no longer sticking to a traditional dinner of meat and two veg; we are all willing to give much more exciting dishes a try. There is a huge demand for new taste sensations that call far-away places to mind. Hot and spicy food is just not so scary anymore.

Supermarkets reflect these changing attitudes. When I started cooking, exotic ingredients that we now think of as commonplace, such as coconut milk and chillies, were hard to come by and involved dedicated scouring of the shelves of specialist shops and delis. Thankfully, nowadays large supermarkets stock most if not all of the ingredients that you'll need for this collection of recipes. I know that sometimes people find the concept of cooking with unusual ingredients slightly intimidating, but do please give it a try. Believe me, once you start to make use of the wonderful range of ingredients now readily available in your local supermarket, you'll be amazed by what you can cook up… and it doesn't have to take you hours, most of the recipes in this book are quick and simple to make.

The fast food industry is also a good indicator of people's foody preferences. Gone are the days when good old fish 'n' chips dominated the take-away market. Now when you're feeling peckish you can grab anything from an authentic Thai to Indian, Mexican, Chinese, Vietnamese… It's all readily available… fantastic! Take-aways aren't the healthiest of options, however, so if you love the flavours, but don't want to pack away the calories, the recipes in this book will help you enjoy the best of both worlds.

In this collection of dishes taken from *In the Kitchen with Ainsley Harriott, Meals in Minutes, Barbecue Bible* and *Big Cook Out*, I've tried to reflect the variety and choice we've grown accustomed to. It's been difficult to narrow the selection down to 100 but I hope I've given you enough curries, stir-frys, wraps, kebabs and skewers, dips and salsas and more to be getting on with.

In the course of my career, I've been lucky enough to travel all over the world in search of new flavours. Many of the recipes featured here were inspired by those travels. They've since become firm family favourites but still never fail to remind me of the place where I first concocted them and the buzz of excitement I felt at exploring new countries and cultures, and meeting new people.

I've tried to keep these recipes relatively simple and quick but have been careful not to compromise on taste. Every dish is bursting with wonderful aromas and exciting flavours so that you can recreate the variety of your local restaurants in your own kitchen.

As for those of you who are as enthusiastic about outdoor cooking as I am, you'll find plenty of recipes that are just perfect for the barbie and entertaining your friends on those long summer days and nights. Conventional cooking methods are provided for most of the barbecue recipes so you can get sizzling in your own kitchen too.

Go on, give my recipes a try and get those tastebuds tingling with a whole range of hot and spicy flavours...

Ainsley Harriott

1 starters

jalapeño chilli-prawn ladders

I first made these in Key West, overlooking the beautiful waters of the Gulf of Mexico. They're great on the barbie but also equally delicious cooked under a hot grill in the kitchen. Go on… get laddering.

I use jalapeño chillies for this because they have a delicate flavour and quite a mild heat. Try to get a variety of colours for this recipe – red, green and yellow.

SERVES 4

8 x 12 CM (4¾ IN) BAMBOO SKEWERS

12 JALAPEÑO CHILLIES, ASSORTED COLOURS

6 FRESH BASIL LEAVES, FINELY SHREDDED

2 CM (¾ IN) PIECE FRESH ROOT GINGER, FINELY CHOPPED

SALT AND FRESHLY GROUND BLACK PEPPER

12 RAW TIGER PRAWNS

A KNOB OF BUTTER

LEMON OR LIME WEDGES AND CHILLED BEER (OPTIONAL), TO SERVE

METHOD

Put the skewers to soak in cold water for 30 minutes.

Slit open the chillies from top to tail, taking care to leave the stalk intact. Scrape out the seeds. Divide the shredded basil and chopped ginger between the chillies and generously season inside.

Shell the prawns, leaving the tail section intact. Place a whole prawn inside each chilli, leaving the tail poking out of the pointed end. Smear a little butter on top of each prawn, then squeeze the chillies together to enclose the prawns.

Thread 3 chillies, alternating the colours, on to 2 short, parallel bamboo skewers so that the chillies look like the rungs of a ladder. Repeat to make 4 ladders.

Cook the chillies under a hot grill or over fairly hot coals for about 5 minutes, turning frequently, until they are softened and a little charred, and the prawns are cooked through.

Serve with a wedge of lemon or lime and chilled beers. Delicious…

chinese crispy spring rolls

These delicious little crispy rolls are ideal as both starter and snack. Spring roll wrappers are now available from major supermarkets or specialist shops.

SERVES 4

2-3 TABLESPOONS VEGETABLE OIL

2 CHINESE LEAVES, FINELY SHREDDED

50 G (2 OZ) TINNED WATER CHESTNUTS, FINELY CHOPPED

1 LARGE CARROT, CUT INTO MATCHSTICKS OR COARSELY GRATED

75 G (3 OZ) BEANSPROUTS

2 SALAD ONIONS, SHREDDED

1 TEASPOON FIVE-SPICE POWDER

½ TEASPOON SUGAR

¼ TEASPOON SALT

2 TABLESPOONS HOISIN SAUCE

12 SPRING ROLL WRAPPERS

1 TEASPOON CORNFLOUR MIXED WITH A LITTLE WATER

SOY SAUCE, TO SERVE

METHOD

Heat 1 tablespoon of the oil in a large wok or frying pan and stir-fry the Chinese leaves, water chestnuts, carrot, beansprouts, salad onions and five-spice over a high heat for 1–2 minutes until beginning to soften.

Stir in the sugar, salt and hoisin sauce and remove from the heat. Set aside to cool slightly.

Open out the spring roll wrappers and place a spoonful of the stir-fried vegetable mixture on each one. Roll up tightly, tucking in the edges, brush the final edge with the cornflour paste, then press down well to seal.

Shallow-fry the spring rolls for 4–5 minutes in the remaining oil, turning occasionally, until crisp and golden. Serve with a little soy sauce for dipping and drizzling.

caribbean plantain rice rings

Plantains are generally longer and thicker than typical eating bananas. They have a lovely slightly sweet, delicate flavour and can be baked, fried or grilled. For this recipe, the plantains should be firm but not too black, which indicates over-ripeness. Be careful when slicing as they can be a bit slippery.

SERVES 4

12 COCKTAIL STICKS

2 LARGE RIPE PLANTAINS

75 G (3 OZ) BUTTER

2 GARLIC CLOVES, PEELED AND CRUSHED

2 SPRING ONIONS, PEELED AND FINELY CHOPPED

3 SMOKED BACK BACON RASHERS, RINDED AND CUT INTO STRIPS

A FEW SPRIGS FRESH THYME

1 SCOTCH BONNET CHILLI, SEEDED AND FINELY CHOPPED

250 G (9 OZ) LONG-GRAIN RICE

1 TABLESPOON TOMATO PURÉE

50 G (2 OZ) CREAMED COCONUT, GRATED

400 ML (14 FL OZ) CHICKEN OR VEGETABLE STOCK

3 WHOLE TOMATOES, SLICED

50 G (2 OZ) CHEESE, GRATED (CHEDDAR AND EDAM WORK WELL)

METHOD

Put the cocktail sticks to soak in cold water for 30 minutes.

Peel the plantains and cut each lengthways into 6 slices about 5mm (¼ in) thick. Heat half the butter in a frying pan, add the plantain strips and fry for about 5 minutes, turning once, until they turn a rich golden brown colour. Drain on a piece of kitchen paper and set aside.

Melt the remaining butter in a saucepan and add the garlic, spring onions and bacon, and fry for about 1–2 minutes. Now add the thyme, chilli, rice, tomato purée and grated coconut. Stir well and when it starts to sizzle, add the chicken or vegetable stock. Bring to the boil, then reduce the heat, cover and simmer for about 15–20 minutes, until the stock has been absorbed and the rice grains are tender.

Curve each slice of plantain into a circle and secure with a cocktail stick. Place on a non-stick baking sheet, then fill the centre with the rice mixture. Arrange a slice of tomato on top of each, followed by a good sprinkling of grated cheese. Place under a medium grill until the cheese has melted.

anaheim chillies
with goats' cheese and black pepper

Believe it or not, these chillies are actually not that much hotter than the average green pepper, and they take on a lovely sweet, charred flavour when they are cooked, much as a pepper would.

SERVES 4

8 LARGE ANAHEIM CHILLIES
100–175 G (4–6 OZ) SOFT GOATS' CHEESE
SALT AND FRESHLY GROUND BLACK PEPPER
½ TABLESPOON OLIVE OIL
GREEN SALAD AND BROWN BREAD, TO SERVE

METHOD

Put the chillies under a hot grill or over medium-hot coals on the barbie for 10–15 minutes, turning now and then, until the skin has blistered and charred and the flesh is just soft. Remove and leave to cool slightly, then carefully scrape off the skin with a small, sharp knife.

Make a cut lengthways down one side of each chilli and scoop out the seeds and the membranes with a teaspoon.

Spread a couple of tablespoons of the cheese into the centre of each one, add a good grind of black pepper, and then push them back into shape.

Brush the outside of the chillies with a little oil, season well with salt and pepper and then place them back under a hot grill or on the barbie for about 4–5 minutes, turning occasionally, until they are heated through and the cheese has started to melt. Serve straight away with a green salad and some delicious brown bread.

roasted aubergine dip

This is one of my wife's favourite dips, and is always made to titillate our friends' taste buds before the grand slam main course.

SERVES 4

2 LARGE AUBERGINES

2 GARLIC CLOVES, PEELED AND CRUSHED

1 SMALL GREEN CHILLI, SEEDED AND FINELY CHOPPED

JUICE OF ½ LEMON

2 TABLESPOONS OLIVE OIL

SALT AND FRESHLY GROUND BLACK PEPPER

1 TABLESPOON CHOPPED FRESH PARSLEY AND CORIANDER

PARSLEY SPRIGS AND LEMON WEDGES, TO GARNISH

PITTA BREAD, CRUSHED GARLIC AND OLIVE OIL, TO SERVE

METHOD

Pre-heat the oven to 190°C/375°F/gas mark 5. Prick the aubergines all over with a fork, cut in half lengthways and place them cut-side down on a lightly greased baking sheet. Bake in the oven for 25–30 minutes until softened and collapsed. Cool slightly.

In a food processor, blitz the garlic, chilli and lemon juice for 10 seconds. Scoop out the aubergine flesh, add to the garlic mixture and blitz again. With the motor still running slowly, add the olive oil in a steady stream until well combined. Alternatively, chop the flesh of the aubergine finely and rub through a sieve, then crush the garlic and chilli with a pestle and mortar and add to the sieved aubergine with the lemon juice. Beat well, then slowly mix in the olive oil, 1 tablespoon at a time, until smooth.

Season with salt and pepper to taste and stir in the parsley and coriander. Spoon on to plates or serve in ramekin dishes. Garnish with parsley and lemon wedges and serve with toasted pitta bread brushed with garlic and olive oil.

crab crunch wraps
with mango chutney

Simple recipes are often the most enjoyable, and this one certainly falls into that category. It's fresh and crunchy with a sweet zing which – dare I say it – is finger-lickin' good. Peri peri seasoning is a Portuguese-style blend of crushed chillies and fragrant herbs, which is available in the spice section of supermarkets and delis.

SERVES 4

75 G (3 OZ) UNSALTED BUTTER

2 SPRING ONIONS, TRIMMED AND FINELY CHOPPED

1 TEASPOON GRATED FRESH ROOT GINGER

75 G (3 OZ) WHITE BREADCRUMBS

120 G (4½ OZ) WHITE CRABMEAT (FRESH, TINNED OR FROZEN),
   WELL DRAINED

½ TEASPOON PERI PERI SEASONING

1 TABLESPOON CHOPPED FRESH CORIANDER

SALT AND FRESHLY GROUND BLACK PEPPER

4 LARGE ICEBERG LETTUCE LEAVES (UNBROKEN)

MANGO CHUTNEY AND 1 FRESH LIME, QUARTERED, TO SERVE

METHOD

Melt the butter in a large frying pan and lightly fry the spring onion and ginger for 30 seconds without letting them colour. Add the breadcrumbs and cook until slightly golden brown. Add the crabmeat, peri peri and coriander. Mix well and correct the seasoning, then remove from the heat.

Lay out the lettuce leaves on a flat surface and place the crab mixture one-third of the way down each leaf. Roll the lettuce over the top of the mixture and fold it in at the sides. Continue to roll until you have a large sausage. Serve immediately on a plate with a good dollop of mango chutney and a wedge of fresh lime.

sticky finger chicken sticks

Chicken wings are inexpensive, cook quickly and make fabulous finger food. Bet you can't eat these without licking your fingers.

SERVES 4

1 TABLESPOON VEGETABLE OIL

1 SMALL ONION, VERY FINELY CHOPPED

2 GARLIC CLOVES, PEELED AND CRUSHED

2 TABLESPOONS CLEAR HONEY

4 TABLESPOONS TOMATO KETCHUP

4 TABLESPOONS WORCESTERSHIRE SAUCE

2 TEASPOONS ENGLISH MUSTARD

2 TEASPOONS TABASCO SAUCE

8 CHICKEN WINGS, TIPS REMOVED

2 TABLESPOONS FLOUR, SEASONED WITH SALT AND PEPPER

METHOD

Pre-heat the oven to 200°C/400°F/gas mark 6.

Heat the oil in a small pan and cook the onion and garlic for 3–4 minutes until softened. Stir in the honey, ketchup, Worcestershire sauce, mustard and Tabasco, and simmer very gently for a minute or so.

Dust the chicken in the seasoned flour, then brush liberally with the sauce, using it all up. Place on a baking sheet and roast for 30 minutes until well browned and cooked through.

Transfer to a serving plate and keep those napkins handy, or just lick those fingers!

grilled guaca mushrooms

This is a lovely starter or perfect for a light lunch or supper. Flat mushrooms are generally large and full of flavour. Some would say they're inferior to other cultivated mushrooms. The opposite is true. They also make a wonderful mushroom soup.

SERVES 4 AS A STARTER OR 2 AS A LIGHT LUNCH

2-3 RASHERS SMOKED STREAKY OR BACK BACON

4 LARGE FLAT MUSHROOMS

SALT AND FRESHLY GROUND BLACK PEPPER

2 TABLESPOONS OLIVE OIL

175 G (6 OZ) CREAM CHEESE

1 TABLESPOON LEMON JUICE

1 GARLIC CLOVE, PEELED AND CRUSHED

1 LARGE RIPE AVOCADO

1 CHILLI, SEEDED AND FINELY CHOPPED

1 LARGE TOMATO, SKINNED, SEEDED AND DICED

25 G (1 OZ) WHITE BREADCRUMBS

25 G (1 OZ) FRESH PARMESAN, FINELY GRATED

2 BUNCHES FRESH WATERCRESS, TO SERVE

METHOD

Grill the bacon until crisp, then set aside. Pre-heat the oven to 220°C/425°F/gas mark 7. Remove the stalks from the mushrooms, chop roughly and place in the upturned caps. Season the mushrooms and drizzle over a little of the olive oil. Pop on to a baking tray and put in the oven for 3–4 minutes. Remove and set on one side.

Put the cream cheese, lemon juice and garlic into a food processor and blitz for 10–15 seconds until fairly smooth. Cut the avocado into quarters, remove the skin and stone, roughly chop the flesh and add to the cream cheese mixture. Season and blitz again for another 10 seconds, then scoop out into a bowl. Chop the bacon into small pieces and add to the guaca mixture, along with the chilli and diced tomato. Mix with a wooden spoon until combined.

Divide the guaca mixture equally between the mushroom caps. Mix together the breadcrumbs and Parmesan, and sprinkle over the mushrooms. Drizzle a little olive oil over each one and add a twist of black pepper. Put under a medium-hot grill until crunchy brown. Serve on a bed of watercress.

caribbean cook-up soup
with dumplings

This gorgeous one-pot soup is so typical of traditional soups throughout the world – anything that's around in the fridge or larder gets thrown in! Yet it always tastes great. I've chosen red kidney beans, but you can use any other variety, such as black-eye, borlotti etc.

SERVES 4

450 G (1 LB) CHICKEN THIGHS

450 G (1 LB) CHUCK OR STEWING STEAK, CUT INTO CHUNKS

SALT AND FRESHLY GROUND BLACK PEPPER

3–4 TABLESPOONS VEGETABLE OIL

1 LARGE ONION, PEELED AND SLICED

2 GARLIC CLOVES, PEELED AND CRUSHED

200 G (7 OZ) YAM, PEELED AND ROUGHLY DICED

1 RED CHILLI, SEEDED AND CHOPPED

A FEW SPRIGS FRESH THYME OR ¼ TEASPOON DRIED THYME

450 G (1 LB) SWEET POTATO, WASHED AND ROUGHLY DICED

1 x 400 G (14 OZ) TIN RED KIDNEY BEANS, DRAINED

1 x 225 G (8 OZ) TIN CHOPPED TOMATOES

5 CM (2 IN) CINNAMON STICK

1¾ LITRES (3 PINTS) BEEF STOCK (USE CUBES)

CHOPPED FRESH PARSLEY, TO GARNISH

FOR THE DUMPLINGS:

350 G (12 OZ) PLAIN FLOUR

100 G (4 OZ) CORNMEAL

¼ TEASPOON DRIED THYME

½ TEASPOON SALT

150–200 ML (5–7 FL OZ) WATER, TO BIND

METHOD

Chop each thigh into two or three pieces. Season the chicken and beef and fry in hot oil for approximately 4–5 minutes until well browned. Add the onion, garlic, yam, chilli, thyme and sweet potato. Stir and cook for another 3–4 minutes. Add the kidney beans, tomatoes and cinnamon stick, then pour in the beef stock. Bring to the boil, then cover and simmer for approx 1 hour until the meat is lovely and tender.

Meanwhile, make the dumplings. Mix all the dry ingredients together and slowly add enough water to make a soft dough. Using floured hands, shape the dough into balls about the size of whole walnuts, then drop them into the soup. Cover with a lid and continue to cook for a further 10–15 minutes until the dumplings have puffed up on the surface of the soup. Adjust the seasoning, sprinkle with chopped parsley and serve.

spicy mean bean dip
with thick plantain crisps

Cooked beans are a very popular ingredient in Jamaica, and here I have turned them into an unusual dip to be served with some crunchy plantain chips. Plantains belong to the same family as the banana, but they must be cooked before they can be eaten. They are sold at various stages of ripeness, and for these crisps you need to use the green, unripe ones.

SERVES 6

400 G (14 OZ) TIN RED KIDNEY OR PINTO BEANS
100 G (4 OZ) SOFT CREAM CHEESE OR GOATS' CHEESE
4 TABLESPOONS SOUR CREAM
1 SMALL RED ONION, VERY FINELY CHOPPED
1 GARLIC CLOVE, PEELED AND CRUSHED
2 TOMATOES, SKINNED, SEEDED AND DICED
2 RED FINGER CHILLIES, SEEDED AND VERY FINELY CHOPPED, OR
  2 TEASPOONS MINCED RED CHILLI FROM A JAR
2 TABLESPOONS CHOPPED FRESH CORIANDER
1 TEASPOON LEMON OR LIME JUICE
SALT AND FRESHLY GROUND BLACK PEPPER

FOR THE PLANTAIN CRISPS:
2 LARGE GREEN PLANTAINS
SUNFLOWER OIL
SEA SALT, TO TASTE

METHOD

Tip the beans into a sieve and rinse off the starchy liquid. Drain them really well, tip them into a bowl and crush into a rough paste with a potato masher.

Mix in the rest of the ingredients, spoon the dip into a bowl, then cover and chill until you are ready to serve.

For the plantain crisps, score the surface of the plantain and peel away the skin. Slice the fruit thinly on the diagonal into a bowl and stir in a little sunflower oil and a little salt. Toss them around a bit with your hands so that all the slices get well coated in the oil.

To cook the crisps on the barbecue, lay them side by side on a fine-meshed rack and cook in batches for about 10 minutes on each side, brushing with a little more oil now and then, until they are crisp and have turned a deep golden brown.

As each batch cooks, tip into a bowl (using oven gloves to hold the mesh rack), and once they are cold, sprinkle them with a little more salt to serve alongside the spicy bean dip.

Alternatively, deep-fry the crisps at 180°C/350°F until crisp and golden. Drain on kitchen paper before sprinkling with the salt, or a little sugar if you like a touch of sweetness.

2 poultry main courses

asian spiced **chicken chompers** ▪ **cajun chicken,** atchafalaya-style ▪ roasted chilli-skin **garlic-stuffed poussins** ▪ **acapulco chicken** tonight ▪ **chicken brummie balti,** alabama-style ▪ **charred chicken brochettes** with sage and red onion ▪ **roasted blackened chicken** chichen-itzá ▪ mexican **chimichangas** ▪ great homemade **chicken burgers** ▪ gorgeous **chicken korma** ▪ **thai coconut chicken** and mango skewers ▪ **chicken roulade** with cream cheese, chilli and garlic ▪ boston bay jamaican **jerk chicken** ▪ **hoisin and honey chicken** stir-fry ▪ balinese **blanket chicken** ▪ **maple-glazed duck** with plum and cinnamon dipping sauce ▪ **spiced duckling** with braised red cabbage and sour cream

asian spiced chicken chompers

These yummy little sticks always go down well at parties. You can prepare the chicken at least 8 hours in advance if you want. For convenience you might want to buy packets of mini chicken fillets instead of breast. Happy chomping!

SERVES 4

8 x 25 CM (10 IN) BAMBOO SKEWERS

4 x 75–100 G (3–4 OZ) SKINLESS, BONELESS CHICKEN BREASTS OR FILLETS

RICE NOODLES OR PLAIN BOILED RICE, AND SWEET CHILLI SAUCE (PAGE 141),
  TO SERVE

FOR THE MARINADE:

1 TEASPOON BLACK PEPPERCORNS

4 GARLIC CLOVES, PEELED

2 TABLESPOONS FRESH CORIANDER LEAVES, PLUS EXTRA, TO GARNISH

1 TEASPOON CASTER SUGAR

JUICE OF 1 LIME

1 TEASPOON FISH SAUCE

1 TEASPOON LIGHT SOY SAUCE

2 TEASPOONS SUNFLOWER OIL

METHOD

Put the skewers to soak in cold water for 30 minutes.

Using a pestle and mortar, grind the peppercorns, garlic and coriander to make a paste. Then mix in the sugar, lime juice, fish sauce, soy sauce and sunflower oil until well blended.

Halve each chicken breast horizontally. Bat each piece out with a rolling pin until 5 mm (¼ in) thick. Cut each piece lengthways into strips 3 cm (1¼ in) wide. Add to the marinade and set aside for about 1 hour.

Thread the chicken strips on to the bamboo skewers and cook under a hot grill for 6–7 minutes on each side or over hot coals for 4–5 minutes on each side, until cooked through and golden brown. Serve with rice noodles or plain boiled rice and my *Sweet Chilli Sauce* for dipping.

cajun chicken, atchafalaya-style

Take a trip down the Atchafalaya River in Cajun country and you'll come across this classic dish. It's a must for all you spicy Cajun connoisseurs. It's simply delicious.

I like to use a whole chicken cut into 8 pieces for this dish as the bones make a lovely stock, but thighs and drumsticks on the bone are just as good. For a fuller flavour cut 3–4 slits in each of the chicken pieces – these allow the sauce to penetrate and reduce cooking time by approximately 10 minutes.

SERVES 4

150 ML (5 FL OZ) CHICKEN STOCK

250 ML (8 FL OZ) TOMATO KETCHUP

100 G (4 OZ) BROWN SUGAR

1 TABLESPOON HOT CHILLI SAUCE

1 TABLESPOON SOY SAUCE

1 TABLESPOON WORCESTERSHIRE SAUCE

1 ONION, FINELY CHOPPED

4 GARLIC CLOVES, PEELED AND CRUSHED

1 TEASPOON PAPRIKA

2 TEASPOONS CHILLI FLAKES

2 TABLESPOONS RED WINE VINEGAR

1 MEDIUM CHICKEN, 1–1.2 KG (2¼–2½ LB), CUT INTO 8 PIECES

2 TABLESPOONS OLIVE OIL

CHIPS, TO SERVE

METHOD

Make a barbecue sauce by placing the chicken stock, tomato ketchup, sugar, chilli sauce, soy sauce, Worcestershire sauce, onion, garlic, paprika, chilli flakes and vinegar in a small pan and simmering together gently for 20 minutes.

Cut 3–4 slits into the chicken pieces, brush them with the oil, then spoon over half the barbecue sauce, rubbing it into the slits and coating the chicken well.

Cook under a medium-hot grill on the lower shelf, or over medium-hot coals on the barbie, for 30–45 minutes, turning occasionally, until the chicken is dark, glossy and cooked through. Serve with a basket of freshly fried chips and the remaining sauce.

roasted chilli-skin
garlic-stuffed poussins

Choose the heat of your hot pepper sauce by varying the type of chilli you use. I prefer a combination of milder jalapeño chillies and Thai birdseye chillies, but the truly brave can always throw in the odd habañero or Scotch bonnet.

SERVES 2

2 x 500 G (1 LB 2 OZ) POUSSINS (BABY CHICKENS)

FOR THE STUFFING:

1 UNPEELED HEAD OF GARLIC

1 RED ONION, CUT INTO 8 WEDGES

1 LIME, CUT INTO 6 WEDGES

2 BAY LEAVES

SALT AND FRESHLY GROUND BLACK PEPPER

2 TABLESPOONS OLIVE OIL

FOR THE HOT PEPPER SAUCE:

6 RED CHILLIES, SEEDED AND ROUGHLY CHOPPED

2 TABLESPOONS RED WINE VINEGAR

3 TABLESPOONS OLIVE OIL

1 SMALL ONION, ROUGHLY CHOPPED

2.5 CM (1 IN) PIECE FRESH ROOT GINGER, FINELY CHOPPED

METHOD

Pre-heat the oven to 200°C/400°F/gas mark 6. To make the stuffing, halve the head of garlic horizontally and place in a small roasting tin with the red onion, lime wedges and bay leaves. Season generously, drizzle with olive oil and roast in the oven, or cook over medium-hot coals, for 25–30 minutes until the garlic is totally soft.

Meanwhile, make the hot pepper sauce. Soak the chopped chillies in the vinegar for 5 minutes–1 hour – the longer the better. Heat the olive oil in a small frying pan and cook the onion for 7–8 minutes until softened and golden. Strain the chillies, reserving the vinegar, and add to the pan with the ginger. Cook for a further 3–4 minutes until the chillies are softened. Blend the chilli mixture in a food processor, or grind with a pestle and mortar to make a coarse paste. Gradually add the reserved vinegar, then season to taste.

Lift the flap of skin at the back of the poussin breasts and gradually loosen it, using your fingers. Spread a couple of teaspoons of the chilli paste under the skin of each bird then stuff the front cavities with the roasted vegetables. Cook in the oven or in a covered barbecue for 40 minutes, turning two or three times. When cooked through and nicely browned, remove from the oven or barbecue.

Serve with the remaining hot pepper sauce.

acapulco chicken tonight

An idea created from lots of leftover broken tortilla chips, and now a family favourite. Even friends request it when coming over for a casual supper. One teaspoon of chilli if you like it hot, two if you like it hot, hot, hot. Can you feel it? Grated cheese sprinkled over the top is a nice touch too.

SERVES 4

1 TABLESPOON VEGETABLE OIL

8 BONELESS, SKINLESS CHICKEN THIGHS, CUT INTO CHUNKS

1 ONION, SLICED

2 GARLIC CLOVES, PEELED AND CHOPPED

1–2 TEASPOONS CHILLI POWDER, PLUS EXTRA FOR SPRINKLING

400 G (14 OZ) TIN CHOPPED TOMATOES

175 ML (6 FL OZ) CHICKEN STOCK

400 G (14 OZ) TIN KIDNEY BEANS, DRAINED

½ TEASPOON DRIED OREGANO

SALT AND FRESHLY GROUND BLACK PEPPER

100 G (4 OZ) TORTILLA CHIPS

SOUR CREAM, PARSLEY SPRIGS AND GRATED CHEESE (OPTIONAL), TO GARNISH

COOKED RICE, TO SERVE

METHOD

Heat the oil in a pan, add the chicken, onion and garlic and cook for about 5 minutes until golden. Add the chilli and stir-fry for 30 seconds, then add the tomatoes, stock, kidney beans and oregano. Season with salt and pepper, bring to the boil, cover and simmer for 20 minutes or until the chicken is tender.

Transfer the chicken mixture to a serving dish and sprinkle over the tortilla chips. Top with a dollop of sour cream, some parsley sprigs, a dusting of chilli powder and a sprinkling of grated cheese (optional). Serve with rice.

chicken brummie balti,
alabama-style

On one of my trips to the USA, I paid a visit to Birmingham, Alabama and thought it might be fun to cook them our Birmingham's most famous dish – the balti. And boy, did they love it… I could probably run for mayor, it got that many votes of approval.

SERVES 4

4 BONELESS, SKINLESS CHICKEN BREASTS, QUARTERED

2 TABLESPOONS VEGETABLE OIL

½ TEASPOON CHILLI POWDER

½ TEASPOON TURMERIC

SALT AND FRESHLY GROUND BLACK PEPPER

1 ONION, FINELY CHOPPED

4 GARLIC CLOVES, PEELED AND FINELY CHOPPED

4 CM (1½ IN) PIECE FRESH ROOT GINGER, FINELY CHOPPED

6 TOMATOES, ROUGHLY CHOPPED

150 ML (5 FL OZ) CHICKEN STOCK

4 TABLESPOONS BALTI CURRY PASTE

1 x 400 G (14 OZ) TIN CHICK PEAS, DRAINED

4 NAAN BREADS

2-3 TABLESPOONS DOUBLE CREAM

2 TABLESPOONS CHOPPED FRESH CORIANDER

LEMON WEDGES, TO SERVE

METHOD

Brush the chicken with a little oil, then dust with chilli powder and turmeric, and season with salt and pepper. Cook in a large frying pan or over medium-hot coals for 3–4 minutes on each side until well browned.

Meanwhile, heat the remaining oil in a balti pan or wok and stir-fry the onion, garlic and ginger for 3–4 minutes until golden. Add the tomatoes, cook for a couple of minutes until they begin to soften, then stir in the stock, curry paste and chick peas.

Add the chicken pieces to the pan or wok and simmer together for 5–8 minutes until the chicken is cooked through.

Briefly warm the naan breads under a hot grill or over the barbecue.

Stir the cream and coriander into the balti and check the seasoning. Divide between serving bowls and serve with lemon wedges and the warm naan.

charred chicken brochettes
with sage and red onion

Brochette is just a fancy name for a kebab, and these juicy skewers well deserve a snazzy title.

SERVES 4

8 BONELESS CHICKEN THIGHS

8 METAL SKEWERS

16 FRESH SAGE LEAVES

2 SMALL RED ONIONS, EACH CUT INTO 8 WEDGES

3 TABLESPOONS OLIVE OIL

1 TEASPOON BALSAMIC VINEGAR

2 GARLIC CLOVES, PEELED AND CRUSHED

½ TEASPOON DRIED CHILLI FLAKES

SALT AND FRESHLY GROUND BLACK PEPPER

SALAD LEAVES, TO SERVE

METHOD

Quarter each chicken thigh and thread on to 8 metal skewers, alternating each piece with a sage leaf or red onion wedge.

Whisk together the olive oil, balsamic vinegar, garlic, chilli flakes and plenty of salt and pepper. Brush the mixture over the brochettes and cook under a pre-heated grill or over medium-low coals for 15–20 minutes, turning occasionally, until the chicken is golden and cooked through, and the red onions are sweet and softened.

Serve on a bed of salad leaves.

roasted blackened chicken
chichen-itzá

A classic barbecue dish, probably as old as the famous ancient pyramid of Chichen-Itzá in southern Mexico.

I really like this recipe because the dry rub on the skin of the chicken blackens to a tasty, crunchy coating during cooking, leaving the flesh inside moist and juicy. How do you like yours?

Why not pop a few jacket potatoes in the oven at the same time?

SERVES 4

2 GARLIC CLOVES, PEELED AND CRUSHED

1 TABLESPOON FRESHLY GROUND BLACK PEPPER

1 TEASPOON DRIED OREGANO

1 TEASPOON DRIED THYME

1 TABLESPOON PAPRIKA

1 TABLESPOON CASTER SUGAR

2 TEASPOONS CHILLI FLAKES

1 TEASPOON ENGLISH MUSTARD POWDER

1 TEASPOON SALT

1 MEDIUM CHICKEN, 1-1.2 KG (2¼-2½ LB), QUARTERED

OLIVE OIL, FOR DRIZZLING

SALAD AND JACKET POTATOES, TO SERVE

METHOD

Mix the garlic, pepper, oregano, thyme, paprika, sugar, chilli, mustard powder and salt together in a large, shallow dish. Roll the chicken quarters in the spice mixture and leave for 5–10 minutes.

Place the chicken on a hot roasting tin. Drizzle a little olive oil over the top of the chicken pieces and cook in a hot oven (200°C/400°F/gas mark 6) for 40–45 minutes until the skin is slightly charred and the meat is cooked through. Alternatively, cook the chicken over medium-hot coals for 30–45 minutes, turning occasionally.

Serve with jacket potatoes and a nice salad.

mexican chimichangas

Chimichangas are simply fried Mexican tortillas that'll get you cha-cha-cha-ing around your kitchen.

SERVES 4

SUNFLOWER OIL, FOR FRYING

1 ONION, FINELY CHOPPED

1 RED PEPPER, SEEDED AND DICED

2 BONELESS, SKINLESS CHICKEN THIGHS, ROUGHLY CHOPPED

2 GREEN CHILLIES, SEEDED AND THINLY SLICED

2 GARLIC CLOVES, PEELED AND FINELY CHOPPED

2 TOMATOES, ROUGHLY CHOPPED

100 G (4 OZ) FROZEN SWEETCORN, THAWED

4 TABLESPOONS TACO SAUCE

4 SALAD ONIONS, FINELY CHOPPED

4 LARGE FLOUR TORTILLAS

COCKTAIL STICKS

TO SERVE:

SHREDDED LETTUCE

SOUR CREAM

READY-MADE GUACAMOLE

METHOD

Heat the sunflower oil in a large pan and stir-fry the onion, pepper and chicken thighs over a high heat for 3–4 minutes until well browned. Stir in the chillies, garlic, tomatoes and sweetcorn and cook for a further 2–3 minutes until the chicken is cooked through.

Stir in the taco sauce and salad onions and set aside to cool a little.

Warm one of the tortillas in a hot, dry frying pan until soft and flexible. Spoon a quarter of the cooled chicken mixture into the centre of the tortilla and fold over the edges to form a neat parcel. Pin in place with cocktail sticks and repeat with the remaining tortillas.

Heat 1 cm (½ in) sunflower oil in a large frying pan and cook the chimichangas for 2–3 minutes on each side until crisp and golden brown. Drain on kitchen paper and serve hot with shredded lettuce, sour cream and guacamole.

great homemade chicken burgers

I don't like shop-bought chicken burgers as they have an unpleasant, synthetic flavour. It's so easy to make tasty ones yourself at home. The chilli is not overpowering but you can exclude it without upsetting the balance of flavours too much.

SERVES 4

500 G (1 LB 2 OZ) MINCED CHICKEN

2 GARLIC CLOVES, PEELED AND CRUSHED

1 RED CHILLI, SEEDED AND FINELY CHOPPED

1 TABLESPOON CHOPPED FRESH MINT

2 TABLESPOONS CHOPPED FRESH PARSLEY OR CORIANDER

2 TEASPOONS WORCESTERSHIRE SAUCE

SALT AND FRESHLY GROUND BLACK PEPPER

OLIVE OIL, FOR BRUSHING

BURGER BUNS OR MUFFINS, SLICED TOMATOES AND MAYONNAISE,
   TO SERVE

METHOD

Mix together the chicken mince, garlic, chilli, herbs, Worcestershire sauce and plenty of salt and pepper.

Shape the mixture into 4 even-sized burgers, then brush lightly with the oil.

Cook under a medium-hot grill, fry in a non-stick frying pan, or slap them on the barbie in the summer for approximately 5 minutes on each side, until browned and cooked through. Serve in burger buns or toasted muffins with sliced tomatoes and mayonnaise. Yum!!

gorgeous chicken korma

My chicken korma is based on a spicy, creamy dish from Kashmir. It's incredibly easy to make and very, very tasty. Chicken korma is popular because the flavours blend together perfectly, leaving that gorgeous taste lingering on your tastebuds 'til the next mouthful. If you have time, allow the chicken to marinate in the korma sauce for up to 2 hours before cooking.

SERVES 4

1 TABLESPOON VEGETABLE OIL

1 ONION, ROUGHLY CHOPPED

350 G (12 OZ) NATURAL YOGHURT

200 ML (7 FL OZ) DOUBLE CREAM

25 G (1 OZ) BUTTER

½ TEASPOON SALT

1 TEASPOON GROUND TURMERIC

2 TEASPOONS HOT CHILLI POWDER

3 GARLIC CLOVES, PEELED AND CRUSHED

3 TABLESPOONS GROUND ALMONDS

4 x 100 G (4 OZ) BONELESS, SKINLESS CHICKEN BREASTS,
   EACH CUT INTO SIX PIECES

TOASTED FLAKED ALMONDS AND CORIANDER SPRIGS,
   TO GARNISH (OPTIONAL)

NAAN BREAD OR RICE, AND CUCUMBER AND RED ONION SALAD,
   TO SERVE

METHOD

Pre-heat the oven to 200°C/400°F/gas mark 6.

Heat the oil in a small pan and cook the onion for 5 minutes until softened. Place in a food processor with the yoghurt, cream, butter, salt, turmeric, chilli, garlic and almonds and whizz until well blended.

Arrange the chicken in a greased casserole dish and pour over the korma mixture. Bake for 30 minutes until the chicken is cooked through. Spoon on to plates, garnish with flaked almonds and coriander sprigs, if you wish, and serve with naan or rice, and salad.

thai coconut chicken
and mango skewers

These gorgeous Thai chicken skewers have a wonderful coconut flavour and a delightful crunch, which comes from the threaded mangetout.

SERVES 4

8 x 25 CM (10 IN) BAMBOO SKEWERS
450 G (1 LB) CHICKEN BREAST FILLETS
1 LARGE, RIPE BUT FIRM MANGO
50 G (2 OZ) MANGETOUT (ABOUT 24)
LIME WEDGES AND NOODLE SALAD, TO SERVE

FOR THE MARINADE:
120 ML (4 FL OZ) TINNED COCONUT MILK
1 TABLESPOON THAI GREEN CURRY PASTE
1 TEASPOON PREPARED MINCED LEMONGRASS FROM A JAR
1 TEASPOON PALM OR LIGHT MUSCOVADO SUGAR
1 TABLESPOON THAI FISH SAUCE
1 TABLESPOON GROUNDNUT OR SUNFLOWER OIL
FINELY GRATED ZEST OF ½ LIME
1 TEASPOON LIME JUICE

METHOD

Put the skewers to soak in cold water for 30 minutes. Cut the chicken into 2.5 cm (1 in) cubes.

Mix together all the marinade ingredients, stir in the chicken and leave it to marinate for 2 hours at room temperature or overnight in the fridge.

Peel the mango and then slice the flesh away from either side of the thin flat stone and cut it into 1 cm (½ in) pieces. Drop the mangetout into a pan of boiling salted water. Bring back to the boil, then drain and refresh under cold running water.

Thread 3 pieces of chicken and 3 mangetout, each folded around a piece of mango, alternately on to a skewer.

Cook the skewers under a medium-hot grill or on the barbie over medium-hot coals for 8–10 minutes, turning occasionally and brushing with the leftover marinade, until the chicken is a little charred and cooked through. Serve with some lime wedges and a crunchy noodle salad.

chicken roulade
with cream cheese, chilli and garlic

A really nice chicken dish that goes down well on those special occasions. You can usually buy the flattened breast in your supermarket, or get your butcher to do it for you. For a special treat, why not use sunblush tomatoes in the sauce, in place of fresh tomatoes.

SERVES 4

4 FLATTENED BONELESS BREASTS OF CHICKEN, INCLUDING FILLETS

125 G (5 OZ) CREAM CHEESE

2 GARLIC CLOVES, PEELED AND CRUSHED

1 RED CHILLI, FINELY CHOPPED

1 TEASPOON SNIPPED CHIVES

SALT AND FRESHLY GROUND BLACK PEPPER

2 TABLESPOONS OLIVE OIL

2 SHALLOTS, FINELY CHOPPED

120 ML (4 FL OZ) WHITE WINE

50 G (2 OZ) BUTTER, SOFTENED

½ TABLESPOON TOMATO PURÉE

1 TABLESPOON CHOPPED FRESH BASIL

1 MEDIUM TOMATO, SKINNED, SEEDED AND DICED,
   OR 5-6 SUNBLUSH TOMATOES, CHOPPED

SNIPPED CHIVES, TO GARNISH

METHOD

Lay the chicken on a flat surface without the fillet (the extra flap of meat attached to the breast). Beat the cream cheese until smooth and add the garlic, chilli, chives and a touch of seasoning. Spread over the breasts, leaving the edges clear. Lay the flattened fillet on top, then roll up, starting with the pointed end and turning the edges in so the filling is sealed in when cooking.

Cut 4 pieces of foil about 15 cm (6 in) square. Brush with a little oil on the shiny side. Put one chicken 'sausage' on each sheet and roll the foil up tightly, twisting the ends firmly to form a tight cylinder. Place in a pan with enough boiling water to cover the sausages and poach for 15–20 minutes until cooked through. If you insert a skewer into the centre of the sausage, the skewer should be hot to touch when it is withdrawn. Switch off the heat and leave the sausages in the water while you make the sauce.

Put the shallots into a pan with the white wine. Bring to the boil and reduce by three-quarters to leave a syrupy glaze. Whisk in the butter off the heat to make a creamy consistency. Add the tomato purée, basil and diced tomato or sunblush tomatoes, and season to taste.

Unwrap the foil from the chicken sausages and make one cut at an angle in each. Spoon a little sauce on to the centre of the plates and lay the chicken pieces on top, slightly overlapping each other. Spoon over the remaining sauce and sprinkle with chives.

boston bay jamaican jerk chicken

Everywhere you go in Jamaica you'll find jerking of some sort, whether it be pork, beef, fish or, indeed, chicken. Everyone's got their favourite recipe. In Boston Bay, Fuzzy, a jerk specialist, added over twenty different ingredients to his jerk pork. Wow! But somehow I think life's too short, so check out my recipe.

Habañeros or Scotch bonnet chillies are the hottest chillies in the world, so go easy. This recipe is quite hot but certainly not overpowering. You can adjust the amount of chillies that you use, or just use a milder type of chilli – after a few goes, you'll soon find a happy medium.

SERVES 6

6 PART-BONED CHICKEN BREASTS OR 18 LARGE CHICKEN WINGS

FOR THE JERK SAUCE:

225 G (8 OZ) ONIONS, QUARTERED

2 HABAÑEROS OR SCOTCH BONNET CHILLIES, HALVED AND SEEDED

50 G (2 OZ) FRESH ROOT GINGER, PEELED AND ROUGHLY CHOPPED

½ TEASPOON GROUND ALLSPICE

THE LEAVES FROM 15 G (½ OZ) FRESH THYME SPRIGS

1 TEASPOON FRESHLY GROUND BLACK PEPPER

120 ML (4 FL OZ) WHITE WINE VINEGAR

120 ML (4 FL OZ) DARK SOY SAUCE

METHOD

Put all the ingredients for the jerk sauce into a food processor and whizz until smooth.

Place the chicken in a large shallow dish, pour over the sauce, cover and leave to marinate in the fridge for 24 hours, turning the chicken every now and then.

Place the chicken breasts under a medium-hot grill, or barbecue over medium-hot coals, for 25–30 minutes, and the wings for 20–25 minutes, turning occasionally and basting now and then with the leftover sauce. As it cooks, the thick sauce will go quite black in places, but as it falls off, it will leave behind a really well-flavoured, crisp skin, with lovely moist, tender meat underneath. Enjoy!

hoisin and honey chicken stir-fry

The secret of a good stir-fry is to have everything prepared in advance, cut roughly into the same size and ready to go into your hot wok at a moment's notice. Remember to keep it hot, hot, hot for that authentic taste.

SERVES 4

1 STICK CELERY
1 CARROT, PEELED
½ RED PEPPER
½ GREEN PEPPER
1 SMALL HEAD BROCCOLI
4 BABY CORN COBS
6 BUTTON MUSHROOMS
2 PLUMP BONELESS CHICKEN BREASTS, CUT INTO STRIPS
   1 CM (½ IN) WIDE AND 7.5 CM (3 IN) LONG
2 TABLESPOONS SOY SAUCE
1 TABLESPOON SESAME OIL
2 TABLESPOONS GROUNDNUT OIL
3 SPRING ONIONS, TRIMMED AND SLICED AT AN ANGLE
1 GARLIC CLOVE, PEELED AND CHOPPED
2.5 CM (1 IN) PIECE FRESH ROOT GINGER, PEELED AND
   FINELY CHOPPED
75 G (3 OZ) BEANSPROUTS
2 TABLESPOONS CLEAR HONEY
2 TABLESPOONS HOISIN SAUCE
2 TABLESPOONS WATER
FRESHLY GROUND BLACK PEPPER
STEAMED RICE OR NOODLES, TO SERVE

METHOD

Cut the celery, carrot, peppers, broccoli, corn cobs and mushrooms horizontally into slices or lengthways into batons.

Mix the chicken with the soy sauce and sesame oil. Heat a wok or large frying pan and then put in the groundnut oil. Swirl around the wok so it is well coated, then add the chicken and stir-fry for 2–3 minutes. Remove with a slotted spoon and keep warm.

Throw the spring onions, garlic and ginger into the wok and fry for 30 seconds, then add the prepared vegetables, except the beansprouts, and continue to stir-fry over a high heat for 2–3 minutes until crisp and tender. Now add the beansprouts, chicken, honey, hoisin sauce and water. Toss, heat for 3–4 minutes, season with pepper and serve with steamed rice or noodles.

balinese blanket chicken

For this recipe, a thick spice and coconut paste is spread under the skin of the chicken instead of over the outside. This helps it to flavour the meat and prevents the tasty paste from over-browning and dropping off during cooking. Go easy when lifting the skin off the chicken, and remember – fingers only. No knives or you'll pierce the skin!

SERVES 6

6 FINE METAL TRUSSING SKEWERS OR COCKTAIL STICKS

5 CM (2 IN) GALANGAL OR FRESH ROOT GINGER, PEELED AND CHOPPED

2 GARLIC CLOVES, PEELED AND CRUSHED

1 LEMONGRASS STALK, ROUGHLY CHOPPED

2 RED BIRDSEYE CHILLIES, SEEDED AND CHOPPED

2 TEASPOONS GROUND TURMERIC

2 TABLESPOONS CHOPPED FRESH CORIANDER

6 SPRING ONIONS, TRIMMED AND CHOPPED

2 FRESH KAFFIR LIME LEAVES, FINELY SHREDDED, OR THE FINELY GRATED ZEST OF 1 LIME

75 G (3 OZ) CREAMED COCONUT

6 PART-BONED CHICKEN BREASTS

METHOD

If using, pre-heat oven to 220°C/425°F/gas mark 7 or heat grill on medium setting. If using cocktail sticks, put them to soak in cold water for 30 minutes.

Put the galangal or root ginger, garlic, lemongrass, chillies, turmeric, coriander, spring onions and lime leaves or lime zest into a food processor and blend to a coarse paste.

Melt the creamed coconut in a small pan, stir in the paste and leave to cool slightly until thickened but not set hard.

Loosen the skin of each chicken breast with your fingers, leaving it attached along one long edge. Spread the paste over the breast meat, lift the skin back into place and secure the open edge with a skewer or cocktail stick.

Cook the chicken in a hot oven, under a medium grill or over medium-hot coals for 20–25 minutes, turning regularly on the grill or barbie until crisp, golden and cooked through. Remove the skewers or cocktail sticks before serving.

maple-glazed duck
with plum and cinnamon dipping sauce

This oriental-style duck is delicious served with the fresh plum and cinnamon sauce. Make sure the duck breasts are not too fatty or ask your butcher to trim them nicely for you. This is also a good recipe to cook on the barbie.

If you don't have any plums, nectarines make a surprisingly good substitute. But me... I'm a plum man meself.

SERVES 4

4 x 150-175 G (5-6 OZ) BONELESS DUCK BREASTS

FOR THE MARINADE:
3 TABLESPOONS MAPLE SYRUP OR CLEAR HONEY
2 TABLESPOONS SOY SAUCE
1 TEASPOON FIVE-SPICE POWDER

FOR THE DIPPING SAUCE:
450 G (1 LB) HALVED AND STONED PLUMS
1 CINNAMON STICK, HALVED
150 ML (5 FL OZ) WHITE WINE
1 BAY LEAF
1 TABLESPOON WINE VINEGAR
2-3 TABLESPOONS LIGHT MUSCOVADO SUGAR
SALT AND FRESHLY GROUND BLACK PEPPER

METHOD

In a shallow bowl, mix together the syrup or honey, soy sauce and five-spice powder. Deeply score the duck skin and add the duck breasts to the marinade, turning to coat the pieces, then set aside for 5 minutes.

Place the plums, cinnamon stick, wine and bay leaf in a small pan on the hob or set over the coals. Simmer gently for 30 minutes until the plums are completely softened.

Meanwhile, heat a frying pan without any oil and, when hot, add the duck, skin-side down first (the duck skin will release fat for frying). Reduce the heat and cook for 8–10 minutes on each side, until browned and cooked through but still a little pink in the centre. Set aside to rest for 5 minutes.

Sieve the sauce and stir in the vinegar, plus sugar, salt and pepper to taste. Spoon into small serving bowls. Carve the duck diagonally and serve with the warm dipping sauce.

spiced duckling
with braised red cabbage and sour cream

This is a very stylish meal, perfect for special occasions. It looks impressive but is really simple to make. It goes down beautifully with a nice spicy red wine, such as Shiraz.

SERVES 2

2 x 100 G (4 OZ) DUCKLING BREASTS
1 TEASPOON MIXED SPICE
½ TEASPOON CAYENNE PEPPER
½ TEASPOON SALT

TO SERVE:
A KNOB OF BUTTER
225 G (8 OZ) RED CABBAGE, SHREDDED
1 SMALL RED ONION, THINLY SLICED
1 TART APPLE, PEELED AND DICED
2 TABLESPOONS LIGHT MUSCOVADO SUGAR
¼ TEASPOON GROUND CINNAMON
120 ML (4 FL OZ) RED WINE
JUICE OF 1 ORANGE
4 TABLESPOONS SOUR CREAM
HANDFUL CHOPPED FRESH HERBS, SUCH AS BASIL, PARSLEY,
    CORIANDER, CHIVES
SALT AND FRESHLY GROUND BLACK PEPPER
MASHED POTATO (OPTIONAL)

METHOD

Score the duck skin in a lattice pattern. Mix the spices and salt in a shallow bowl and add the duck, using your fingertips to rub in the spices.

Cook the duck, skin-side down first, in a hot chargrill pan or frying pan for 7 minutes on each side until browned and cooked through but still a little pink in the centre. Remove from the pan and place on a warm plate to rest for 5 minutes.

Meanwhile, melt the butter in a wok or deep frying pan and stir-fry the cabbage over a high heat for 1–2 minutes. Add the red onion and apple and cook for a further 1–2 minutes. Stir in the sugar and cinnamon and cook, stirring, until the sugar dissolves. Add the wine and orange juice and simmer gently for 10 minutes until the vegetables and apple are tender.

Meanwhile, stir together the sour cream and fresh herbs and season to taste. Spoon the cabbage on to serving plates. Slice the duck breasts and fan out on top of the cabbage. Garnish with a spoonful of herby cream and serve immediately. A side order of mashed potato never goes amiss.

3 lamb main courses

shepherd's pie with a curry kick ■ **butterfly leg of lamb** with a chilli mustard crust ■ **spiced mazatlán meatballs** ■ **braised yukatán lamb** in foil purses ■ **lamb chops** with olive tapenade and a parmesan crust ■ **peppered lamb patties** ■ **shish kebabs** with mint, cucumber and yoghurt dressing ■ **moroccan lamb,** lemon and onion kebabs ■ **lamb fillets** with spiced harissa yoghurt ■ **marinated lamb skewers** with fresh mint chutney ■ **lemon and herb lamb** with ginger rice

shepherd's pie with a curry kick

Shepherd's pie is such a lovely old-fashioned dish. Here I've kicked it up to great effect with a touch of spicy curry paste. When mashing the potatoes, use electric beaters, if you have them, for perfect results.

SERVES 2-3

450 G (1 LB) FLOURY POTATOES, DICED

2 TABLESPOONS SUNFLOWER OIL

1 SMALL ONION, FINELY CHOPPED

1 GARLIC CLOVE, PEELED AND FINELY CHOPPED

1 LARGE CARROT, DICED

300 G (11 OZ) MINCED LAMB

2 TABLESPOONS MILD CURRY PASTE

250 ML (8 FL OZ) HOT LAMB STOCK

1 TABLESPOON TOMATO KETCHUP

2 TEASPOONS DARK SOY SAUCE

1 TEASPOON CORNFLOUR

50 G (2 OZ) FROZEN PEAS, THAWED

2 TOMATOES, ROUGHLY CHOPPED

SALT AND FRESHLY GROUND BLACK PEPPER

2 TABLESPOONS MILK

A KNOB OF BUTTER

25 G (1 OZ) MATURE CHEDDAR, GRATED

METHOD

Cook the potatoes in a large pan of boiling, salted water for 8–10 minutes until tender.

Heat 1 tablespoon of sunflower oil in a large frying pan and cook the onion, garlic, carrot and mince for 3–4 minutes until well browned. Stir in the curry paste, stock, tomato ketchup and soy sauce. Bring to the boil and simmer rapidly for 3–4 minutes. Mix the cornflour to a paste with a little water and stir into the pan with the peas and chopped tomatoes and bring back to the boil, stirring until slightly thickened. Season with salt and pepper to taste.

Drain the potatoes well and return to the pan. Mash well, then beat in the milk and butter until smooth and creamy. Season to taste.

Pre-heat the grill to medium. Spoon the mince mixture into a heatproof pie dish and spoon over the mashed potato. Using a fork, mark a criss-cross pattern on the top.

Sprinkle over the cheddar and place under the grill for 3 minutes until the cheese melts and the pie is speckled with brown. Spoon on to plates and serve.

butterfly leg of lamb
with a chilli mustard crust

Save time on marinating your meat – just rub on this mustard mix and let it crust up in the oven or over the coals.

This recipe uses butterflied leg of lamb, which has had its bone removed and then been opened flat. It's easy enough to do it yourself but a lot easier to ask your butcher to do it for you.

SERVES 10

3 TABLESPOONS DIJON MUSTARD

1 TABLESPOON PLAIN FLOUR

1 TABLESPOON SOY SAUCE

1 TABLESPOON HOT CHILLI SAUCE

1 TABLESPOON OLIVE OIL

2 TEASPOONS FINELY CHOPPED FRESH ROSEMARY

½ TEASPOON SALT

½ TEASPOON FRESHLY GROUND BLACK PEPPER

2 KG (4½ LB) BUTTERFLIED LEG OF LAMB

METHOD

If using, pre-heat the oven to 220°C/425°F/gas mark 7.

Mix together the mustard, flour, soy sauce, chilli sauce, olive oil, rosemary, salt and pepper to make a smooth, thick paste.

Smear the paste all over the lamb, then cook in the oven or over medium coals for 40 minutes, turning every 10–15 minutes until crusty and browned on the surface but still a little pink in the centre. Serve immediately.

spiced mazatlán meatballs

These delicious, moist little meatballs, delicately flavoured with spices from the Middle East, taste brilliant topped with yoghurt and red onion and rolled up in soft, warm flatbread. You can also make them into sausage shapes for a change, and the addition of some thinly sliced cucumber is also nice.

SERVES 4

500 G (1 LB 2 OZ) LEAN MINCED LAMB

A PINCH OF SALT

1 ONION, FINELY CHOPPED

2 TEASPOONS GROUND CUMIN

1 TEASPOON GROUND ALLSPICE

¼ TEASPOON CAYENNE PEPPER

4 TABLESPOONS ROUGHLY CHOPPED FRESH CORIANDER

TO SERVE:

4 MIDDLE EASTERN FLATBREADS OR PLAIN NAAN

1 RED ONION, THINLY SLICED

1 x 200 G (7 OZ) CARTON GREEK YOGHURT

1 LEMON, CUT INTO WEDGES

METHOD

Gently heat a large non-stick frying pan. Place the lamb, salt, onion, cumin, allspice, cayenne and coriander in a food processor and whizz until well blended. Using wet hands, shape the mixture into 20 meatballs and cook in a non-stick frying pan or over hot coals for 10 minutes, turning frequently until well browned.

Warm the flatbreads in the oven or microwave for 1–2 minutes on each side until softened and warmed through.

Scatter the red onion over the flatbreads and spoon a dollop of yoghurt on each. Arrange 5 meatballs on top of each, then roll into a cone shape. Serve each with a lemon wedge.

braised yucatán lamb in foil purses

A classic dish from the Yucatán region of Mexico. You can actually get something very similar to this dish from one of the many local restaurants in the area, although they load it with enough chilli to blow your head off. Pre-boiling the garlic takes the edge off the strong taste.

I've used shoulder of lamb but, if you wish, you can use leg. It's a more expensive cut, but is less fatty and should be cooked for about 30–40 minutes.

SERVES 4

4 UNPEELED GARLIC CLOVES

1.5 KG (3 LB) BONELESS SHOULDER OF LAMB, CUBED

2 LARGE TOMATOES, DICED

3 TABLESPOONS MALT VINEGAR

2 FRESH CHILLIES, SEEDED AND FINELY CHOPPED,
    OR 1½ TEASPOONS CHILLI POWDER

2 TEASPOONS BROWN SUGAR

1 TABLESPOON PAPRIKA

1 TEASPOON DRIED OREGANO

½ TEASPOON DRIED THYME

½ TEASPOON SALT

½ TEASPOON FRESHLY GROUND BLACK PEPPER

WARM TORTILLAS AND SHREDDED SALAD, TO SERVE

METHOD

Pre-heat the oven to 220°C/425°F/gas mark 7. Boil the garlic cloves in a little water for 3–4 minutes, take out and put to one side.

Place the lamb and tomatoes in a large bowl. In another, smaller bowl, mix together the vinegar, chillies or chilli powder, sugar, paprika, oregano, thyme, salt and pepper. Peel the garlic cloves and crush them into the spice mixture. Add the spice mixture to the meat and tomatoes and toss together well.

Divide the mixture between 4 large, extra-strong squares of foil and scrunch the edges together at the top like a wigwam. Place the parcels on a baking sheet and cook in the oven for 45 minutes–1 hour, gently shaking the parcels once or twice during cooking until the meat is tender. Alternatively, cook over medium-hot coals for about 1–1½ hours.

Give each diner a parcel to open out at the table and serve with warm tortillas and shredded salad.

lamb chops
with olive tapenade and a parmesan crust

The beauty of this recipe is that you can cook it either on a barbecue (make sure the rack is not too widely spaced) or indoors in a frying pan with a little olive oil and foaming butter. Either way it's simply and totally scrumptious.

SERVES 4

12 LAMB CHOPS

SALT AND FRESHLY GROUND BLACK PEPPER

2 TABLESPOONS BLACK OLIVE PASTE

2 TABLESPOONS SEASONED FLOUR

2 EGGS, BEATEN

1 TABLESPOON SNIPPED FRESH CHIVES

8 TABLESPOONS DRIED BREADCRUMBS

1 TABLESPOON FRESHLY GRATED PARMESAN

OLIVE OIL, FOR FRYING OR BRUSHING

A KNOB OF BUTTER

MASHED POTATO AND MIXED SALAD, TO SERVE

METHOD

Season the chops with salt and pepper. Thinly spread the black olive paste on both sides, then dust very lightly with seasoned flour.

Whisk together the eggs, chives and a little seasoning. In a separate shallow dish, mix together the breadcrumbs and Parmesan.

Dip the floured chops in the beaten egg, then coat well in the breadcrumb mixture, gently shaking off any excess crumbs.

Add a couple of tablespoons of light olive oil and a knob of butter to your frying pan over a medium heat. When the butter has melted, add the breaded chops and cook for 3–4 minutes on each side until golden. Alternatively, brush a barbecue rack with a little oil and cook the chops over medium-hot coals for 5 minutes on each side. Serve with mashed potato and a nice salad.

peppered lamb patties

If you like that warm, peppery taste, this is for you. I've coated these juicy lamb burgers in crushed peppercorns, just like a peppered steak.

SERVES 4

500 G (1 LB 2 OZ) MINCED LAMB

1 BUNCH SALAD ONIONS, FINELY CHOPPED

2 GARLIC CLOVES, PEELED AND FINELY CHOPPED

1 TABLESPOON CHILLI SAUCE

½ TEASPOON SALT

1 TABLESPOON DIJON MUSTARD

2 TABLESPOONS COARSELY CRUSHED BLACK PEPPERCORNS

OIL, FOR BRUSHING

SALAD AND CHIPS, TO SERVE

METHOD

Place the lamb, salad onions, garlic, chilli sauce and salt in a large bowl and mix together well. Shape the mixture into 4 even-sized burgers, then smear both sides with a little mustard.

Sprinkle with peppercorns, then cook in a heated chargrill pan brushed with a little oil or under a pre-heated grill for 3–4 minutes on each side until crusted and golden on the outside but still a little pink in the centre. Serve with salad and chips.

shish kebabs
with mint, cucumber and yoghurt dressing

The dip that goes with these kebabs is simply a combination of cucumber and tomato, but that doesn't sound half as exciting or sexy as it tastes. This dish is also super served cold.

SERVES 4

12 x 25 CM (10 IN) BAMBOO SKEWERS

450 G (1 LB) MINCED LAMB

1 SMALL ONION, FINELY CHOPPED

3 TABLESPOONS CHOPPED FRESH MINT

1 TABLESPOON CHOPPED FRESH OREGANO

1 TABLESPOON CHOPPED FRESH PARSLEY

½ TEASPOON MIXED SPICE

½ TEASPOON GROUND CORIANDER

½ TEASPOON GROUND CUMIN

SALT AND FRESHLY GROUND BLACK PEPPER

450 G (1 LB) SMALL NEW POTATOES

½ SMALL CUCUMBER

150 G (5 OZ) CARTON NATURAL YOGHURT

1 TOMATO, SEEDED AND DICED

¼ TEASPOON GARLIC POWDER OR 1 GARLIC CLOVE, PEELED AND CRUSHED

4 PITTA BREADS, PLUS WEDGES OF CUCUMBER, TOMATO AND LEMON,
    TO SERVE

METHOD

Put the skewers to soak in cold water for 30 minutes. Pre-heat the grill to high.

Mix together the lamb, onion, 1 tablespoon of mint, the oregano, parsley, mixed spice, coriander and cumin and season with salt and pepper. Divide the mixture into 12 and squeeze around 12 skewers.

Cook the potatoes in boiling, salted water for 10–15 minutes or until tender.

Grill the lamb kebabs for 8–10 minutes, turning occasionally until well browned. Meanwhile, grate the cucumber, squeeze out the excess liquid with your hands and mix with the yoghurt, tomato, 1 tablespoon of mint and the garlic, and season with salt and pepper.

Drain the potatoes and toss with the remaining mint. Serve the lamb with potatoes, pitta bread, a dollop of the yoghurt mixture and wedges of fresh cucumber and tomato, and a wedge of lemon.

moroccan lamb, lemon and onion kebabs

The spices in this dish are very typical of those found all over North Africa. Harissa is a fiery red chilli paste from this region but you can replace it with minced red chilli in a jar. This recipe really creeps up on you – an absolute winner every time.

SERVES 4

900 G (2 LB) BONED SHOULDER OR LEG OF LAMB

3 TABLESPOONS OLIVE OIL

2 TABLESPOONS LEMON JUICE

1 TEASPOON GROUND CORIANDER

1 TEASPOON GROUND CUMIN

½ TEASPOON GROUND TURMERIC

½ TABLESPOON PAPRIKA

1 GARLIC CLOVE, PEELED AND CRUSHED

1 TEASPOON HARISSA PASTE OR MINCED RED CHILLI FROM A JAR

SALT AND FRESHLY GROUND BLACK PEPPER

1 SMALL RED ONION

1 SMALL LEMON

4 x 30 CM (12 IN) FLAT METAL SKEWERS

COUSCOUS, TO SERVE

METHOD

Trim any excess fat off the outside of the lamb and then cut it into roughly 5 cm (2 in) chunks. Place in a bowl with the olive oil, lemon juice, coriander, spices, garlic, harissa paste or minced red chilli and some seasoning and mix together well. Cover and leave to marinate at room temperature for 2 hours or overnight in the fridge.

Peel the onion, leaving the root end intact, then cut it into 8 wedges so that the slices of onion stay together at the root. Cut each lemon into 8 wedges.

Thread the lamb, lemon and onion wedges alternately on to the skewers and cook under a medium-hot grill, or barbecue over medium-hot coals, for about 10–15 minutes, turning them now and then, until they are nicely browned on the outside but still pink in the centre. Serve with couscous.

lamb fillets with spiced harissa yoghurt

If you marinate any meat in yoghurt, it becomes unbelievably tender, and when you add plenty of spices, garlic and chilli, it's incredibly tasty too.

SERVES 4

1 TABLESPOON GARAM MASALA OR MILD CURRY PASTE

PINCH OF GROUND CARDAMOM (OPTIONAL)

½ TEASPOON SALT

2 GARLIC CLOVES, PEELED AND CRUSHED

1 TABLESPOON HARISSA PASTE OR MINCED RED CHILLI FROM A JAR

1 TEASPOON LEMON JUICE

200 G (7 OZ) GREEK YOGHURT

4 x 175 G (6 OZ) OR 2 x 350 G (12 OZ) LAMB FILLETS, TRIMMED

2 TABLESPOONS SUNFLOWER OIL

1 TABLESPOON BLACK MUSTARD SEEDS

2 ONIONS, THINLY SLICED

SALT AND FRESHLY GROUND BLACK PEPPER

TO SERVE:

4 TOMATOES, SLICED

1 SMALL RED ONION, THINLY SLICED INTO RINGS

1 TEASPOON ROASTED CUMIN SEEDS

1 TEASPOON LEMON JUICE

4 MINI NAAN BREAD OR 2 LARGE BREADS, CUT IN HALF LENGTHWAYS

METHOD

Mix the garam masala or curry paste, ground cardamom, salt, 2 crushed garlic cloves, harissa or red chilli paste and lemon juice into the yoghurt. Lightly score the outside of the lamb fillets, lay them in a shallow, non-metallic dish and pour over the yoghurt mixture. Rub the mixture into the lamb really well, cover and leave to marinate at room temperature for 1 hour or overnight in the fridge.

Heat the oil in a large pan. Add the mustard seeds and, as soon as they start to pop, add the onions and fry over a medium heat, stirring now and then, until they are richly golden. Stir in the rest of the garlic, season with a little salt and pepper and cook for 2–3 minutes. Set aside and keep warm.

Layer the tomatoes and red onions in a shallow dish, sprinkling each layer with some of the roasted cumin seeds, lemon juice, salt and pepper. Set to one side.

Cook the marinated fillets in a heated chargrill pan or over medium-hot coals for 4–5 minutes on each side for medium-rare lamb.

Sprinkle the naan bread on both sides with a little water and heat through in the chargrill pan or under a grill.

Transfer the lamb fillets to a board and cut diagonally into thick slices. Place the lamb, naan bread and fried onions on 4 plates and serve with the tomato salad.

marinated lamb skewers
with fresh mint chutney

The sun is shining, the days are long. What better reason do you need to light up a barbecue? So here's a dish that'll keep them coming back again and again. And if it's winter, just grill the kebabs instead.

SERVES 3-4

8 x 25 CM (10 IN) BAMBOO SKEWERS
1 BONED LEG OF LAMB (ABOUT 1.5 KG/2-3 LB)
PITTA BREAD, TO SERVE

FOR THE MARINADE:
2 GARLIC CLOVES, PEELED AND CRUSHED
2.5 CM (1 IN) PIECE FRESH ROOT GINGER, PEELED AND GRATED
1 TEASPOON CHOPPED FRESH CORIANDER
1 TEASPOON TURMERIC
1 TEASPOON GROUND CUMIN
1 TEASPOON MILD CURRY PASTE OR CRUSHED DRIED CURRY LEAVES
1 TABLESPOON SOY SAUCE
1 TABLESPOON LEMON JUICE
1 TABLESPOON LIGHT SESAME OIL
2 TABLESPOONS OLIVE OIL
SALT AND FRESHLY GROUND BLACK PEPPER

FOR THE CHUTNEY:
1 LARGE BUNCH FRESH MINT
3 TABLESPOONS LEMON JUICE
175 G (6 OZ) PINE NUTS
3 TABLESPOONS CLEAR HONEY
1 RED CHILLI, SEEDED AND FINELY CHOPPED
1 TABLESPOON CRUSHED BLACK PEPPERCORNS

METHOD

Put the skewers to soak in cold water for 30 minutes.

Trim the meat, removing all the sinew and excess fat, and cut into 2.5 cm (1 in) cubes. Mix all the marinade ingredients together, pour over the cubes of lamb and marinate for 2–4 hours, or overnight if you are organized. If you put the lamb mixture in the fridge to marinate, make sure it's covered so that the smell doesn't affect other foods.

To make the chutney, put the ingredients into a food processor and blitz in short bursts.

Thread the meat on to skewers, 6–8 per stick, and arrange them on a wire rack set over a baking tray. Grill for 8–10 minutes, turning frequently, until nicely browned, still juicy and slightly pink in the centre. Alternatively, barbecue for 10–15 minutes, turning every 3–4 minutes until sizzling brown on all sides. Serve with warmed, split pitta bread and spoon over the mint chutney.

lemon and herb lamb
with ginger rice

I'm particularly fond of lamb. Perhaps it's something to do with its subtle sweetness. This dish is full of Oriental flavours and style.

SERVES 4

1 TEASPOON GROUND FENNEL OR CUMIN

1 GARLIC CLOVE, PEELED AND CRUSHED

1 TABLESPOON CHOPPED FRESH ROSEMARY, OR 1 TEASPOON
   DRIED ROSEMARY

1 TEASPOON EACH GRATED LEMON ZEST AND JUICE

3 TABLESPOONS OLIVE OIL

1 TABLESPOON SOY SAUCE

1 ONION, SLICED

2 GARLIC CLOVES, FINELY CHOPPED

2 CM (¾ IN) PIECE FRESH ROOT GINGER, FINELY CHOPPED

200 G (7 OZ) LONG-GRAIN RICE

100 G (4 OZ) BUTTON MUSHROOMS, SLICED

450 ML (15 FL OZ) HOT VEGETABLE STOCK

½ TEASPOON GROUND TURMERIC

4 x 100 G (4 OZ) BONELESS CHUMP, LEG OR SHOULDER LAMB STEAKS

2 TABLESPOONS CHOPPED FRESH CORIANDER OR PARSLEY

SALT AND FRESHLY GROUND BLACK PEPPER

½ CUCUMBER, SEEDED AND CUT INTO STRIPS, TO GARNISH

METHOD

Stir together the fennel or cumin, garlic, rosemary, lemon zest and juice, 2 tablespoons of the oil, and the soy sauce. Set aside.

Heat the remaining oil in a pan and cook the onion, garlic and ginger for 4–5 minutes until softened and golden. Stir in the rice and cook, stirring, for 1 minute. Add the mushrooms, stock and turmeric and bring to the boil. Cover and simmer gently for 15 minutes until the liquid is absorbed and the rice is tender.

Pre-heat the grill to high. Brush the lamb with the soy sauce mixture, then grill for 4 minutes. Turn, brush with more soy sauce mixture and cook for 3–4 minutes longer until crispy and tender. Stir the coriander or parsley into the rice and season. Spoon the rice on to serving plates, slice the lamb into strips and arrange on top of the rice. Garnish with fine strips of cucumber.

4 pork main courses

peri peri pork and lemon medallions ■ smoky **chinese-style ribs** ■ beer and chilli **rack of ribs** ■ **pork palenque strips** with avocado tacos ■ clare's chinese **crispy belly pork** ■ **smoked gammon** with honey, ginger and pineapple salsa ■ chorizo cheese and potato **quesadillas** ■ asian teriyaki **belly of pork** ■ **asian-style mince** with fragrant thai rice ■ **chinese char sui** lettuce rolls ■ marvellous chilli-cheese **meatballs** ■ maple-glazed **pork spare ribs** ■ south east asian **roast pork** ■ **mediterranean pork burgers** ■ **chicago deli pizza** on the stone ■ smoked bacon and bean **ranch pasties**

peri peri pork and lemon medallions

Peri peri chilli sauce is a Portuguese condiment which is also popular in Brazil and part of Africa. It is sometimes known as piri piri or pili pili, and is often served with chicken or fish, though I like it best with pork. Peri peri sauce is now available in most supermarkets.

The pork medallions should be about the same size as the lemon slices, so you might have to flatten them out with a mallet or the palm of your hand.

SERVES 4

8 COCKTAIL STICKS
2 LEMONS
VEGETABLE OIL, FOR FRYING OR BRUSHING
500 G (1 LB 2 OZ) PORK FILLET
6 TABLESPOONS PERI PERI SAUCE
SALAD AND FLATBREADS, TO SERVE

METHOD

Put the cocktail sticks to soak in cold water for 30 minutes.

Very thinly slice the lemons and brush lightly with oil. Cut the pork fillet into 8 rounds 1 cm (½ in) thick and brush with 1 tablespoon of the peri peri sauce.

Place a lemon slice on top of each piece of pork and pin in place with a cocktail stick. Cook the medallions, lemon-side down first, in a heated frying pan with 2 tablespoons of oil, or cook over hot coals for 2–3 minutes on each side until well browned and cooked through.

Arrange on a serving platter with a little bowl of the remaining sauce for drizzling over. Have plenty of salad and flatbread to hand.

smoky chinese-style ribs

Try this delicious marinade with any type of pork on the bone – the shoulder blade is particularly good.

SERVES 4

2 GARLIC CLOVES, PEELED AND CRUSHED

½ TEASPOON SALT

4 TABLESPOONS CASTER SUGAR

1 TABLESPOON HOISIN SAUCE

1 TABLESPOON YELLOW BEAN SAUCE

2 TABLESPOONS SOY SAUCE

1 TABLESPOON SHAOXING RICE WINE OR DRY SHERRY

A FEW DROPS OF RED FOOD COLOURING

1 SHEET PORK RIBS (ABOUT 675 G/1 LB 7 OZ)

METHOD

Mix together the garlic, salt, sugar, hoisin sauce, yellow bean sauce, soy sauce, rice wine or sherry, and food colouring.

Place the ribs in a roasting tin and pour over the marinade. Refrigerate for an hour or so, basting occasionally with the marinade.

Cook the ribs under a pre-heated grill or over medium coals for about 40 minutes, turning occasionally and brushing over the remaining marinade, until cooked through. Carve between the ribs and serve.

beer and chilli rack of ribs

I first made these in Dodge City, USA, dressed up just like the outlaw Jesse James. Yes, I felt like a right old jesse, but the ribs were a knock-out, as you'll discover.

The beer marinade used in this delicious dish tenderizes the meat, making for really juicy ribs.

SERVES 4

1 x 330 ML (11½ FL OZ) BOTTLE STRONG LAGER

GRATED ZEST AND JUICE OF 1 LIME

2 GARLIC CLOVES, PEELED AND CRUSHED

2 TEASPOONS CHOPPED FRESH THYME

2 TABLESPOONS DARK MUSCOVADO SUGAR

1 HOT, SMOKED CHILLI (E.G. CHIPOTLE), CRUSHED, OR 1 TEASPOON
  CHILLI FLAKES

SALT AND FRESHLY GROUND BLACK PEPPER

1 SHEET PORK RIBS (ABOUT 750 G/1½ LB)

METHOD

Mix together the beer, lime zest and juice, garlic, thyme, sugar, chilli and plenty of seasoning.

Add the ribs to the beer mixture and leave to marinate for 8–24 hours in the fridge.

Cook the rack of ribs on a wire rack in a hot oven or over medium-hot coals for 25–35 minutes (don't forget to place a tray underneath to catch all the juices). Turn the ribs occasionally, until they're well browned and cooked through.

Yep! These really are flamin' tasty and no stickiness, y'all.

pork palenque strips
with avocado tacos

I make this the traditional Mexican way by slow-barbecuing, or even slow-roasting, the pork and then slicing it into thin strips. This recipe is also a great way to use up cold pork left over from a roast. If tacos are not available, use tortilla wraps or pitta bread.

SERVES 6

1 KG (2¼ LB) BONED, ROLLED SHOULDER OR LEG OF PORK

SALT AND FRESHLY GROUND BLACK PEPPER

1 TABLESPOON VEGETABLE OIL

1 LARGE ONION, FINELY CHOPPED

4 TOMATOES, ROUGHLY CHOPPED

2 DRIED SMOKED CHILLIES (E.G. CHIPOTLE), FINELY CHOPPED, OR A GOOD
   PINCH OF CHILLI FLAKES

4 TABLESPOONS CHOPPED FRESH CORIANDER

1 x 400 G (14 OZ) TIN KIDNEY BEANS

TO SERVE:

6 TACO SHELLS

BUNCH OF SALAD ONIONS, FINELY SLICED

2 AVOCADOS, SKINNED, STONED AND FINELY DICED

LIME WEDGES, TO GARNISH

SOUR CREAM (OPTIONAL)

METHOD

Season the pork with salt and pepper and cook in an oven preheated to 180°C/350°F/gas mark 4 or in a covered barbecue over low-medium coals, for 2 hours until well browned and cooked through.

Allow the pork to cool, then slice very thinly. Break the slices into long strips.

Heat the oil in a large pan and cook the onion for 3–4 minutes until beginning to soften.

Stir in the chopped tomatoes, chillies and coriander and cook for 5 minutes. Add the pork and season to taste.

Meanwhile, gently heat the beans in a small pan, then roughly mash.

Briefly warm the taco shells under a medium grill or over hot coals, then divide the mashed beans between them. Pile the pork mixture on top, sprinkle over the salad onions and avocado dice and serve each with a lime wedge for squeezing over.

A drizzle of sour cream can really add to the experience…

clare's chinese crispy belly pork

Now here's one of my wife Clare's favourites. This is an easy way to make lovely, crispy Chinese-style pork, which looks particularly dramatic and exciting on the barbecue. Go on, pop some bubbles. You won't be disappointed.

SERVES 6

APPROXIMATELY 1.5 LITRES (2½ PINTS) BOILING WATER

1.5 KG (3 LB) SHEET BELLY PORK

2 TABLESPOONS SALT

2 TABLESPOONS SOY SAUCE

2 TEASPOONS FIVE-SPICE POWDER

STIR FRIED UDON NOODLES (PAGE 139), TO SERVE

FOR THE SAUCE:

3 TABLESPOONS SOY SAUCE

3 TABLESPOONS DRY SHERRY

1 TABLESPOON DARK BROWN SUGAR

A PINCH OF DRIED CHILLI FLAKES

2 CM (¾ IN) PIECE FRESH ROOT GINGER, FINELY CHOPPED

METHOD

Pour a kettleful of boiling water over the skin of the pork and pat dry with kitchen paper. Rub the salt into the pork fat and leave to dry for 45 minutes.

Wipe the excess salt off the pork with kitchen paper, then, using a small, sharp knife, deeply score the pork skin in a criss-cross lattice. Turn the meat over and pierce the flesh in several places with a skewer. Rub the soy sauce and five-spice powder into the pork and set aside to marinate for an hour or so.

Roast on a rack in an oven pre-heated to 220°C/425°F/gas mark 7 for 25–30 minutes until the crackling is crunchy and the pork is cooked through. Alternatively, cook over medium-hot coals, skin-side down first, for 30 minutes on each side.

Meanwhile, make the sauce. Heat the soy, sherry, sugar, chilli and ginger together in a small pan, stirring until the sugar dissolves. Remove from the heat and allow to cool.

Slap the crispy bubbled pork on to a chopping board and cut into slices 2 cm (¾ in) wide. Transfer to a platter, and serve with *Stir-fried Udon Noodles* and the dipping sauce.

smoked gammon
with honey, ginger and pineapple salsa

Treat yourself to a real feast and serve these sticky gammon steaks with baked potatoes, a dollop of sour cream and corn on the cob.

SERVES 2

2 x 175 G (6 OZ) SMOKED GAMMON STEAKS
5 CM (2 IN) PIECE FRESH ROOT GINGER
1 TABLESPOON CLEAR HONEY
1 TEASPOON SOY SAUCE
1 TABLESPOON VEGETABLE OIL

FOR THE SALSA:
1 x 250 G (9 OZ) FRESH PINEAPPLE
1 TABLESPOON VEGETABLE OIL
JUICE OF 1 ORANGE
2 TABLESPOONS LIGHT MUSCOVADO SUGAR
1 GARLIC CLOVE, PEELED AND CRUSHED
2 TABLESPOONS WINE VINEGAR
4 SALAD ONIONS, FINELY CHOPPED
2 RED CHILLIES, SEEDED AND FINELY CHOPPED
10 FRESH BASIL LEAVES, SHREDDED
SALT AND FRESHLY GROUND BLACK PEPPER

METHOD

To make the salsa, cut the top and bottom off the pineapple, then slice off the skin. Cut the pineapple into 8 even-sized wedges. Cook the wedges in a large-ridged chargrill pan over a high heat for 2–3 minutes on each side, until lightly charred. Alternatively, brush the wedges with the oil and barbecue over hot coals for 3–4 minutes on each side.

Mix together the orange juice, sugar, garlic, vinegar, salad onions and chillies in a large bowl. Cut the pineapple wedges widthways into chunks, stir into the mixture, then allow to cool a little.

Meanwhile, using a small pointed knife, make about 8 small slits in each gammon steak. Peel the ginger and cut into 16 thin pieces. Push a piece of ginger right into each slit so that it is visible on either side of the steak.

Whisk together the honey, soy sauce and oil and brush over the gammon. Cook the gammon steaks under a hot grill for 5–6 minutes on each side, or over medium coals for 8–10 minutes on each side, until cooked through, shiny and a little charred around the edges.

Stir the basil into the salsa and season to taste. Arrange the gammon steaks on a plate and pile on the salsa.

chorizo cheese and potato
quesadillas

These really are great and, if you get organized before your guests arrive, they can do the final bit of cooking for themselves.

SERVES 4

1 TEASPOON VEGETABLE OIL

1 SMALL ONION, FINELY CHOPPED

2 GARLIC CLOVES, PEELED AND FINELY CHOPPED

2 GREEN CHILLIES, SEEDED AND CUT INTO THIN STRIPS

100 G (4 OZ) CHORIZO SAUSAGE, ROUGHLY CHOPPED

225 G (8 OZ) COOKED POTATOES, COARSELY MASHED

150 G (5 OZ) CHEDDAR OR OTHER TASTY CHEESE, GRATED

2 TABLESPOONS CHOPPED FRESH CORIANDER

SALT AND FRESHLY GROUND BLACK PEPPER

8 CORN OR FLOUR TORTILLAS

SOUR CREAM AND SWEET CHILLI SAUCE (PAGE 141), TO SERVE

METHOD

Heat the oil in a pan and cook the onion, garlic and chillies for 2–3 minutes until softened. Add the chorizo and cook for a further couple of minutes until the sausage is dark and crispy.

Add the potato, stirring until heated through. Remove from the heat, stir in the cheese and coriander and season to taste.

Heat two or three tortillas at a time on the barbecue or one at a time in a large, non-stick frying pan. Spread some of the potato mixture on top, then quickly fold into quarters. Cook for a minute or so on each side until crisp and golden brown, then wrap in a paper napkin.

Ripple together a little sour cream and *Sweet Chilli Sauce* and dollop a small spoonful on top of each quesadilla.

asian teriyaki belly of pork

This dish has a truly oriental flavour because it includes a ready-made Japanese teriyaki sauce.

SERVES 4

700 G (1 LB 7 OZ) PIECE OF BELLY PORK ONCE THE SKIN AND BONES
   HAVE BEEN REMOVED
STEAMED RICE, TO SERVE

FOR THE MARINADE:
2.5 CM (1 INCH) FRESH ROOT GINGER, PEELED
75 ML (3 FL OZ) BOTTLED TERIYAKI MARINADE
1 TABLESPOON DARK SOY SAUCE
4 TABLESPOONS CLEAR HONEY
2 TABLESPOONS CHILLI SAUCE
2 TEASPOONS SESAME OIL
1 GARLIC CLOVE, PEELED AND CRUSHED

METHOD

Cut the belly pork into 4 pieces. Make shallow, diagonal cuts, no more than 3 mm (⅛ in) deep, across both sides of the meat.

Finely grate the ginger on to a plate and squeeze out the juice into a shallow non-metallic dish. Discard the ginger.

Stir in the rest of the marinade ingredients and then add the pork. Turn it over a few times so that it is well coated in the marinade, cover and leave at room temperature for 2 hours or for up to 24 hours in the fridge, turning it every now and then.

Cook under a medium-hot grill or over medium-hot coals for approximately 6–8 minutes on each side, turning a few times and basting repeatedly with the leftover marinade, until it has taken on a rich, glossy brown colour on the outside but is still moist and juicy in the centre. Serve with plain steamed rice.

asian-style mince
with fragrant thai rice

This puts a spicy spin on the traditional bolognese. For extra authenticity, serve with Thai fragrant rice.

SERVES 4

250 G (9 OZ) LONG-GRAIN OR THAI FRAGRANT RICE

1 TABLESPOON VEGETABLE OIL

1 ONION, HALVED AND SLICED

1 GARLIC CLOVE, PEELED AND CHOPPED

1 RED PEPPER, SEEDED AND ROUGHLY CHOPPED

450 G (1 LB) PORK MINCE

½ TEASPOON CHILLI POWDER

2 TABLESPOONS DARK SOY SAUCE

175 ML (6 FL OZ) CHICKEN STOCK

2 TEASPOONS CORNFLOUR

FRESHLY GROUND BLACK PEPPER

A HANDFUL OF FRESH BASIL LEAVES

METHOD

Cook the rice in a pan of boiling water for about 15 minutes. Meanwhile, heat the oil in a pan and cook the onion for 3–4 minutes until golden. Stir in the garlic and pepper and cook for 4 minutes, then add the mince and chilli powder and cook for 2–3 minutes until well browned. Stir in the soy sauce and stock, bring to the boil and simmer for a good 5 minutes.

Blend the cornflour with 1 tablespoon of water until smooth, add to the pan and stir until slightly thickened. Season with pepper and stir in the whole basil leaves. Drain the rice and spoon on to plates, top with the mince and serve.

chinese char sui lettuce rolls

Char sui is the name for that infamous 'red' roast pork dish that you can get in almost every Chinese restaurant. Here I have served it carved into thin slices, rolled up inside lettuce leaves with crunchy spring onions and cucumber strips.

SERVES 4

2 x 450 G (1 LB) PORK FILLETS

5 CM (2 IN) FRESH ROOT GINGER, PEELED

1 LARGE GARLIC CLOVE, PEELED AND CRUSHED

2 TABLESPOONS HOISIN SAUCE

2 TABLESPOONS DARK SOY SAUCE

2 TEASPOONS LIGHT SOFT BROWN SUGAR

1 TEASPOON FIVE-SPICE POWDER

2 TABLESPOONS SUNFLOWER OIL

4–6 DROPS RED FOOD COLOURING (OPTIONAL)

2 TABLESPOONS CLEAR HONEY

OIL, FOR FRYING

TO SERVE:

½ CUCUMBER

6 SPRING ONIONS, TRIMMED

1 LARGE ICEBERG LETTUCE, BROKEN INTO LEAVES

12 TABLESPOONS CHINESE PLUM SAUCE

METHOD

If using, pre-heat the oven to 200°C/400°F/gas mark 6. Trim any fat and membrane off the outside of the pork fillets.

Finely grate the ginger and squeeze out the juice into a shallow non-metallic dish. Discard the ginger. Stir in the rest of the marinade ingredients. Add the pork fillets and coat them well. Cover and set aside in the fridge for at least 2 hours.

Cut the cucumber in half lengthways and scoop out the seeds with a teaspoon. Cut into thin strips about 7.5 cm (3 in) long. Halve the spring onions and cut lengthways into very thin shreds. Arrange on a serving plate in separate piles along with the lettuce leaves and a small bowl of plum sauce.

Heat a little oil in a frying pan and sear the pork all over until well browned. Transfer to a roasting tin and drizzle over any pan juices. Roast for 35 minutes, basting occasionally with any remaining marinade. Alternatively, barbecue the pork fillets over medium-hot coals for about 20 minutes, turning now and then and basting with the leftover marinade, until the juices run clear when the meat is pierced with a skewer.

Transfer the pork to a board, carve it into thin slices and pile it on to a warmed serving plate. Instruct everyone to take a lettuce leaf and place a line of cucumber strips, spring onion and pork down the centre. Then spoon over a little plum sauce, roll the lettuce leaf up into a parcel and eat!

marvellous chilli-cheese
meatballs

My meatballs are marvellous! Well, so the wife keeps telling me. What do you think? I've made them with pork, but any lean mince will do just as well. You could also serve the meatballs with other types of pasta, such as linguine, spaghettini, taglioni or fettucine, to name but a few.

SERVES 2

225 G (8 OZ) LEAN MINCED PORK

4 SALAD ONIONS, FINELY CHOPPED

2 GARLIC CLOVES, PEELED AND FINELY CHOPPED

1 RED CHILLI, SEEDED AND FINELY CHOPPED

2 TABLESPOONS FRESHLY GRATED PARMESAN, PLUS EXTRA TO SERVE

2 TEASPOONS FRESH THYME LEAVES

SALT AND FRESHLY GROUND BLACK PEPPER

1 TABLESPOON OLIVE OIL

100 ML (3½ FL OZ) RED WINE

150 G (5 OZ) SPAGHETTI OR TAGLIATELLE

400 G (14 OZ) TIN CHOPPED TOMATOES

1 DRIED BAY LEAF

PINCH OF SUGAR

METHOD

Mix together the mince, salad onions, garlic, chilli, Parmesan, thyme and plenty of salt and pepper. Shape into 12 small, firm balls. Heat the oil in a large pan and cook the meatballs for 3–4 minutes, shaking the pan frequently, until well browned. Pour in the red wine and bubble vigorously for 1–2 minutes.

Cook the pasta in a large pan of salted water according to packet instructions. Stir the chopped tomatoes, bay leaf, sugar, and salt and pepper into the meatballs. Bring to the boil and simmer for 8–10 minutes until the meatballs are cooked through.

Drain the pasta and return to the pan. Spoon in some of the tomato sauce and toss well together. Transfer to large serving bowls and spoon over the chilli-cheese meatballs with the sauce. Sprinkle liberally with Parmesan and serve.

maple-glazed pork spare ribs

Unfortunately, most supermarkets sell single ribs, but if you can get them in racks from a butcher, it will make things much easier and quicker when you come to turn them over. Pre-cooking them in the oven, or boiling them in water with a teaspoon of mixed herbs, before glazing them ensures that they will be really nice and fall-off-the-bone tender at the end.

SERVES 4

2 KG (4½ LB) MEATY PORK SPARE RIBS, IN 2 OR 3 RACKS IF POSSIBLE

FOR THE GLAZE:

150 ML (5 FL OZ) MAPLE SYRUP

¼ TEASPOON CAYENNE PEPPER

½ TEASPOON SALT

½ TEASPOON FRESHLY GROUND BLACK PEPPER

2 GARLIC CLOVES, CRUSHED

2 TABLESPOONS TOMATO PURÉE

1 TABLESPOON DIJON MUSTARD

2 TABLESPOONS LEMON JUICE

METHOD

Pre-heat the oven to 190°C/375°F/gas mark 5. Lay the ribs in a large, foil-lined roasting tin and cook for 45 minutes until tender, or pre-boil for 30 minutes in a saucepan of water. The ribs can be set aside at this stage until you are ready to finish them, if you wish.

Mix the remaining ingredients together in a bowl.

Brush the ribs with some of the glaze and barbecue over medium-hot coals for 10–15 minutes, turning them now and then and basting with more of the glaze, until they are tender and lightly browned. Alternatively, pre-heat the grill until hot. Arrange the glazed ribs in a foil-lined roasting tin and grill for 15 minutes, turning and basting frequently.

Give them one last coating of glaze so that they are nice and sticky, transfer them to a board and cut between the bones into single ribs. Serve with plenty of napkins and finger bowls to hand – but you'll be sucking those fingers regardless.

south east asian roast pork

There's rather a lot going on in this recipe, but it's well worth the effort as the end result is a mouth-watering experience. Ask your butcher for a skinned and rolled loin of pork called the 'eye' of the meat. You can either cook it in the oven or in a kettle barbecue, which adds a lovely smoky taste.

SERVES 6

900 G (2 LB) BONED, SKINNED AND ROLLED LOIN OF PORK

2 TABLESPOONS SUNFLOWER OIL

½ TEASPOON PREPARED TAMARIND FROM A JAR

1 TEASPOON PREPARED MINCED LEMONGRASS FROM A JAR

120 ML (4 FL OZ) WATER

75 ML (3 FL OZ) TINNED COCONUT MILK

½ TABLESPOON PALM OR LIGHT MUSCOVADO SUGAR

¼ TEASPOON SALT

FOR THE DRY MARINADE:

1 TEASPOON EACH CHOPPED FRESH CORIANDER AND FRESH BASIL

1 TEASPOON DESICCATED COCONUT

½ TEASPOON GROUND TURMERIC

1 TEASPOON HOT CHILLI POWDER

1 TABLESPOON PALM OR LIGHT MUSCOVADO SUGAR

½ TEASPOON SALT

FOR THE WET MARINADE:

1 GREEN FINGER CHILLI, SEEDED AND ROUGHLY CHOPPED

2 GARLIC CLOVES, PEELED

2 SHALLOTS OR ½ SMALL RED ONION

25 G (1 OZ) GROUND ALMONDS

25 G (1 OZ) FRESH ROOT GINGER, PEELED AND ROUGHLY CHOPPED

1 FRESH KAFFIR LIME LEAF OR 1 STRIP PARED LIME ZEST, CHOPPED

METHOD

Mix the dry marinade ingredients together in a bowl. Add pork and coat well. Set aside for 1 hour. Blend wet marinade ingredients to a smooth paste in a food processor.

Heat the oil in a frying pan. Add the wet marinade, tamarind and lemongrass and fry for about 3 minutes until the mixture splits away from the oil. Add the water and simmer for 2 minutes. Add the coconut milk, sugar and salt and simmer for a further 2 minutes. Taste the sauce and adjust the seasoning.

Pour the wet marinade over the pork and coat well. Place the pork on a rack sitting inside a roasting tray, then cook in an oven pre-heated to 200°C/400°F/gas mark 6 or in a covered barbecue for 1-1¼ hours, spooning over the wet marinade every 15–20 minutes, until the juices run clear when the centre of the pork is pierced with a thin skewer. Leave the pork, covered with a sheet of foil, to relax for 5 minutes on a board before serving.

mediterranean pork burgers

This dish has all my favourite Mediterranean flavours in it: pine nuts, basil, sun-dried tomatoes, garlic and Parmesan – delicious.

SERVES 4

500 G (1 LB 2 OZ) GOOD-QUALITY SAUSAGEMEAT

8 SUN-DRIED OR SUNBLUSHED TOMATOES IN OIL, VERY FINELY CHOPPED

2 GARLIC CLOVES, PEELED AND FINELY CHOPPED

2 TABLESPOONS FRESHLY GRATED PARMESAN

2 TABLESPOONS TOASTED PINE NUTS, ROUGHLY CHOPPED

2 TABLESPOONS EACH CHOPPED FRESH BASIL AND PARSLEY

SALT AND FRESHLY GROUND BLACK PEPPER

ITALIAN BREAD, CORN COBS, LIME WEDGES AND CRAZY CRUNCHY CRISPY
   COLESLAW (PAGE 134), TO SERVE

METHOD

Place the sausagemeat in a large bowl and stir in the sun-dried tomatoes, garlic, Parmesan, pine nuts, basil, parsley and plenty of seasoning.

Using damp hands, shape the mixture into 4 even-sized burgers. Cook on a heated chargrill pan or over medium coals for 5–6 minutes on each side until well browned and completely cooked through. Serve with Italian bread, such as ciabatta, corn cobs, *Crazy Crunchy Crispy Coleslaw*, lime wedges, and a hearty red wine.

chicago deli pizza on the stone

I first cooked this while I was in Chicago, the home of American pizza. Well... so they say. The pizza stone I used was bought from a local cookshop, and it gave a really good, crispy base. These stones are not expensive and I definitely recommend them – just make sure that the one you buy can withstand high temperatures, as some types may crack under the intense heat of the barbecue. They also work really well in a domestic oven.

MAKES 2 LARGE PIZZAS

450 G (1 LB) STRONG WHITE BREAD FLOUR, PLUS EXTRA FOR DUSTING

1 TEASPOON EASY-BLEND DRIED YEAST

1 TEASPOON SALT

2 TABLESPOONS CHOPPED FRESH PARSLEY

2–3 TABLESPOONS OLIVE OIL

300 ML (10 FL OZ) WARM WATER

SELECTION OF TOPPINGS, SUCH AS CHORIZO SAUSAGE, MARINATED
VEGETABLES, SMOKED CHEESE, OLIVES AND CAPERS

FOR THE SAUCE:

6 FRESH TOMATOES, ROUGHLY CHOPPED

2 GARLIC CLOVES, PEELED AND FINELY CHOPPED

½ TEASPOON DRIED OREGANO

2 TABLESPOONS OLIVE OIL

2 TABLESPOONS TOMATO KETCHUP

SALT AND FRESHLY GROUND BLACK PEPPER

METHOD

Sift the flour into a bowl and add the yeast and salt. Make a well in the centre and add the parsley, oil and warm water to make a soft dough. Knead the dough for 10 minutes until smooth and elastic. Rub a little oil into the surface of the dough, cover with plastic wrap and leave in a warm place for an hour or so until doubled in size.

Set a pizza stone or sturdy baking sheet in a hot oven pre-heated to 230°C/450°F/gas mark 8, or set the stone directly on the warm coals, and leave to heat up for 15 minutes. Dust generously with flour.

Meanwhile, make the sauce. Place the tomatoes, garlic, oregano, oil and ketchup in a small pan and heat gently for 10–15 minutes until thickened and pulpy. Season to taste.

Roll the dough into 2 circles 30 cm (12 in) in diameter and place on the stone or baking sheet.

Spoon the fresh tomato sauce over the dough and arrange your choice of toppings on the pizzas. Cook for 15–20 minutes until the dough is crisp and cooked through, then serve.

smoked bacon and bean
ranch pasties

These really are packed full of flavour, and the kids just love 'em – so does my wife, Clare, too. If the baked beans have too much sauce when you open the can, drain some of it off, so the filling is not too sloppy.

SERVES 4

1 TABLESPOON SUNFLOWER OIL

4 RASHERS SMOKED STREAKY BACON, CUT INTO STRIPS

1 SMALL ONION, FINELY CHOPPED

1 GARLIC CLOVE, PEELED AND FINELY CHOPPED

200 G (7 OZ) TIN BAKED BEANS

50 G (2 OZ) MATURE CHEDDAR, FINELY DICED

A FEW DROPS OF TABASCO SAUCE

375 G (13 OZ) PACK READY-ROLLED PUFF PASTRY

MILK, FOR BRUSHING

MIXED LEAF SALAD, TO SERVE

METHOD

Pre-heat the oven to 220°C/425°F/gas mark 7. Heat the oil in a small pan and cook the bacon, onion and garlic for 4–5 minutes until golden. Remove from the heat and mix with the baked beans and diced cheese. Add Tabasco to taste.

Open out the pastry and cut into quarters to give four 20 x 11 cm (8 x 4½ in) rectangles. Spoon the filling into the centre of each, then bring up the edges to enclose the filling. Press the edges together to create a seam across the centre of each pasty. Transfer to a baking sheet, brush with a little milk and bake for 12–15 minutes until puffed and golden brown.

Serve with salad and watch them disappear.

5

beef main courses

sirloin steak **fajitas burritos** ■ surf and turf **barbecue skewers** ■ spiced **lemon-rub steak** with charred tomato salsa ■ **asado beef fillet** with fiery hot sauce ■ **steaks** with anchovy-pepper dressing ■ seared **thai beef salad** ■ **golden empanadas**

sirloin steak fajitas burritos

This is a cross between Mexican-style sizzling fajitas and tortilla burritos and it works a treat. If I'm making it for my kids, I sometimes throw a handful of grated cheese into each parcel so that they're scrumptiously melty and oozy when cut open.

SERVES 2

300 G (11 OZ) SIRLOIN STEAK

1 ORANGE PEPPER, CUT LENGTHWAYS INTO 1 CM (½ IN) WIDE STRIPS

1 RED ONION, CUT INTO 8 WEDGES

½ TEASPOON DRIED OREGANO

½ TEASPOON FENNEL SEEDS

1 TABLESPOON SUNFLOWER OIL

SALT AND FRESHLY GROUND BLACK PEPPER

4 x 20 CM (8 IN) FLOUR TORTILLAS

1 x 150 ML (5 FL OZ) CARTON SOUR CREAM OR GUACAMOLE

COCKTAIL STICKS

SUNFLOWER OIL, FOR BRUSHING

SALAD, TO SERVE

METHOD

Cut the sirloin steak into strips 1 cm (½ in) wide. Place the pepper, onion, oregano, fennel seeds and sunflower oil in a bowl. Season generously and toss well together.

Cook the pepper strips and red onion in a large frying pan for 5 minutes, turning occasionally until they begin to soften and char. Add the steak strips and cook for 1–2 minutes on each side until browned. Remove the peppers, onions and steak and set aside.

Briefly warm 1 tortilla in a non-stick frying pan for just a few seconds on each side until it is soft and will fold without cracking.

Spoon a quarter of the steak mixture on to the tortilla and top with a spoonful of sour cream or guacamole. Fold the edges over to enclose the filling and make a neat, square package. Skewer on either side with a cocktail stick to secure. Repeat with the other 3 tortillas.

Brush the parcels with a little of the sunflower oil and return to the heated frying pan for 2–3 minutes on each side until crisp and golden brown. Serve hot with plenty of salad.

surf and turf barbecue skewers

This unusually named dish comes from Australia, where they serve prawns from the 'surf' or sea, together with steak reared on the 'turf'. Unlikely as it may seem, they actually go together really well, especially when they are both smothered with a yummy garlic and parsley butter. Now, anyone for a swim, or a stroll in the grass?

SERVES 4

4 x 25 CM (10 IN) BAMBOO SKEWERS

350 G (12 OZ) PIECE OF SIRLOIN OR RUMP STEAK,
   CUT 2.5 CM (1 IN) THICK

12 HEADLESS RAW TIGER PRAWNS

3 TABLESPOONS OLIVE OIL

2 GARLIC CLOVES, PEELED AND CRUSHED

1 TEASPOON PAPRIKA

¼ TEASPOON TABASCO SAUCE

½ TEASPOON WORCESTERSHIRE SAUCE

SALT AND FRESHLY GROUND BLACK PEPPER

BREAD, TO SERVE

FOR THE GARLIC AND PARSLEY BUTTER:

50 G (2 OZ) BUTTER

2 GARLIC CLOVES, PEELED AND CRUSHED

2 TABLESPOONS CHOPPED FRESH PARSLEY

FINELY GRATED ZEST OF ½ LEMON

1 TABLESPOON LEMON JUICE

METHOD

Put the skewers to soak in cold water for 30 minutes.

Cut the steak into roughly 16 x 2.5 cm (1 in) cubes. Peel the prawns, leaving the tail segment in place.

Mix the olive oil with the garlic, paprika, Tabasco, Worcestershire sauce and plenty of salt and pepper. Dip the prawns into the marinade, lift out and set aside on a plate.

Stir the cubes of steak into the marinade and leave for 15 minutes.

Thread 4 pieces of steak and 3 prawns alternately on to the skewers and cook in a chargrill pan or over medium-hot coals for 5–10 minutes, turning every now and then, until the steak is done to your liking and the prawns are just cooked through.

Meanwhile, put the butter and garlic into a small pan and melt. Add the chopped parsley, lemon zest and lemon juice.

As soon as the kebabs are cooked, lift them on to 4 plates, spoon over the garlic butter and serve with some nice bread.

spiced lemon-rub steak
with charred tomato salsa

To remove the skin from the tomatoes when making the salsa, insert a fork into the base of the tomato and hold over an open flame turning slowly. Alternatively, roast in a hot oven for approximately 4–5 minutes, or cut in half and cook cut-side down on the barbecue until softened and a little charred. Then peel off skins and roughly chop.

SERVES 2

GRATED ZEST OF 1 LEMON

2 GARLIC CLOVES, PEELED

½ TEASPOON BLACK PEPPERCORNS

½ TEASPOON CUMIN SEEDS

1 TEASPOON DRIED OREGANO

½ TEASPOON CAYENNE PEPPER

½ TEASPOON COARSE SEA SALT

2 x 175 G (6 OZ) SIRLOIN STEAKS

FOR THE SALSA:

A SMALL BUNCH OF FRESH CORIANDER

A SMALL BUNCH OF FRESH MINT

3 PLUM TOMATOES, SKINNED AND ROUGHLY CHOPPED

1 RED ONION, FINELY CHOPPED

1 FRESH GREEN CHILLI, FINELY CHOPPED

2 TABLESPOONS OLIVE OIL

JUICE OF ½ LEMON

ROCK SALT AND FRESHLY GROUND BLACK PEPPER

LEAFY SALAD, TO SERVE

METHOD

Using a pestle and mortar, a mini food processor or a coffee grinder, grind the lemon zest, garlic, peppercorns and cumin seeds together until well blended. Add the oregano, cayenne and salt and grind again. Rub the mixture into the meat. Set aside for an hour or two.

Finely chop the herbs and mix with the chopped tomatoes, onion, chilli, olive oil and lemon juice. Season well to taste.

Heat a chargrill pan and cook the steaks for 3–4 minutes on each side. Serve each with a good dollop of charred tomato salsa and a leafy green salad. Wow!

asado beef fillet with fiery hot sauce

Asado is the Argentinian word for 'barbecue' and is particularly associated with Patagonia in the southern part of the country, where the legendary South American horsemen, the gauchos, cook their meat on open fires.

SERVES 6

1 x 1 KG (2¼ LB) FILLET OF BEEF

1 TABLESPOON OLIVE OIL

2 TEASPOONS DRIED ROSEMARY

FOR THE HOT SAUCE:

1 LARGE ONION, FINELY CHOPPED

2 TOMATOES, SEEDED AND FINELY CHOPPED

1 GREEN PEPPER, SEEDED AND FINELY CHOPPED

2 HOT RED CHILLIES, SEEDED AND FINELY CHOPPED

100 ML (3½ FL OZ) RED WINE VINEGAR

1-2 TABLESPOONS CASTER SUGAR

2 TABLESPOONS OLIVE OIL

SALT AND FRESHLY GROUND BLACK PEPPER

METHOD

Begin by making the hot sauce. Stir together the onion, tomatoes, green pepper, chillies, vinegar, sugar to taste, olive oil and plenty of seasoning. Set aside at room temperature for at least an hour.

Brush the meat with the olive oil. Season generously and sprinkle with the rosemary.

Pre-heat the grill to hot. Place the beef fillet on a wire rack set over a baking tray. Grill for 25 minutes, turning once for rare, or 30 minutes, turning once for medium. Alternatively, cook the beef over medium coals, turning occasionally, for 30–60 minutes, according to how well done you like it.

Allow the meat to rest for a good 5 minutes, then carve and serve with the hot sauce.

steaks with anchovy-pepper dressing

Steak and anchovy sounds like an odd combination, but this tastes fantastic. I once knocked this up in Buenos Aires using the most amazing Argentinian beef, and it was a great hit. I love to serve it sandwiched between two slices of bread or, if I feel like really treating myself, I top it with a fried egg for a great breakfast.

SERVES 4

6 TABLESPOONS OLIVE OIL

2 TABLESPOONS RED WINE VINEGAR

6 ANCHOVIES IN OLIVE OIL, FINELY CHOPPED

½ TEASPOON FRESHLY GROUND BLACK PEPPER

ROCK SALT AND FRESHLY GROUND BLACK PEPPER

12 x 50 G (2 OZ) VERY THINLY SLICED FILLET STEAKS

2 TABLESPOONS FINELY CHOPPED FRESH PARSLEY

GREEN SALAD AND BREAD, TO SERVE

METHOD

Place the oil, vinegar, anchovies and pepper in a small pan and simmer gently for 2–3 minutes on the stove or on the side of the barbie.

Meanwhile, season the steaks and cook in a pre-heated chargrill pan or over very hot coals for 30 seconds on each side, then transfer to serving plates.

Stir the parsley into the oil mixture and pour over the steaks. Serve with a green salad and plenty of bread to mop up the juices.

seared thai beef salad

The people of Thailand and neighbouring countries are very fond of those semi-clear, slightly spicy sauces, and this one is drizzled over thin slices of tender, medium-rare steak and served with a crunchy lettuce salad.

SERVES 4

750 G (1½ LB) PIECE OF SIRLOIN STEAK, CUT 5 CM (2 IN) THICK

JUICE OF 1 LIME

2 TEASPOONS PALM OR LIGHT MUSCOVADO SUGAR

SALT AND GROUND SICHUAN PEPPER

FOR THE SALAD:

1 CRISP LETTUCE SUCH AS COS, ROMAINE OR ICEBERG

½ CUCUMBER

3 TOMATOES, SKINNED, QUARTERED AND SEEDED

1 RED ONION, HALVED AND THINLY SLICED

LEAVES FROM A SMALL BUNCH OF FRESH CORIANDER

FOR THE DRESSING:

4 TABLESPOONS LIME JUICE

4 TABLESPOONS THAI FISH SAUCE

1-2 RED BIRDSEYE CHILLIES, SEEDED AND THINLY SLICED

1 STALK OF LEMONGRASS, OUTER LEAVES REMOVED AND THE CORE VERY FINELY CHOPPED

2 GARLIC CLOVES, PEELED AND VERY FINELY CHOPPED

2 SPRING ONIONS, TRIMMED AND VERY THINLY SLICED

2 TABLESPOONS CHOPPED FRESH MINT

1 TABLESPOON PALM OR LIGHT MUSCOVADO SUGAR

METHOD

Start by preparing the salad. Break the lettuce into leaves, wash and dry well. Tear them into large pieces and place into a salad bowl.

Peel the cucumber, cut it in half lengthways and scoop out the seeds with a teaspoon. Slice across into thin half-moons.

Cut the tomatoes into thin crescent-shaped pieces.

Add the cucumber, tomatoes, onion and coriander leaves to the lettuce and toss together. Transfer to a large serving plate and leave in the fridge to chill.

Mix together all the ingredients for the dressing and set aside.

Sprinkle the steak on both sides with the lime juice and sugar, then season with some salt and Sichuan pepper.

Cook in a chargrill pan or over medium-hot coals for 25–30 minutes, turning frequently, until well browned on the outside but still rare and juicy in the centre. Transfer to a board, cover with a sheet of foil and leave to rest for 10 minutes.

Carve the steak into thin slices and arrange in the centre of the chilled salad leaves. Spoon over the dressing and serve immediately.

golden empanadas

Empanadas are spicy Argentinian patties. Serve with a nice relish such as *Chimichurri* (page 140) or, dare I say, brown sauce.

SERVES 6

500 G (1 LB 2 OZ) PLAIN FLOUR

¼ TEASPOON SALT

125 G (4½ OZ) BUTTER, MELTED

1 EGG, BEATEN

200 ML (7 FL OZ) WARM WATER

FOR THE FILLING:

1 TABLESPOON VEGETABLE OIL

350 G (12 OZ) MINCED BEEF

4 SALAD ONIONS, FINELY CHOPPED

1 TABLESPOON PAPRIKA

½ TEASPOON DRIED CHILLI FLAKES

2 TABLESPOONS TOMATO PURÉE

¼ TEASPOON GROUND CUMIN

50 G (2 OZ) SMALL SEEDLESS RAISINS

2 HARD-BOILED EGGS, ROUGHLY CHOPPED

50 G (2 OZ) STONED GREEN OLIVES, ROUGHLY CHOPPED

SALT AND FRESHLY GROUND BLACK PEPPER

VEGETABLE OIL, FOR FRYING

METHOD

To make the dough, sift the flour and salt into a large bowl. Stir in the butter and half the egg, then gradually work in enough warm water to make a firm dough. Knead vigorously for 5–10 minutes until the dough is smooth. Cover it with a cloth and allow it to rest for 15–30 minutes.

For the filling, heat the oil in a large pan and cook the beef, salad onions and paprika for 4–5 minutes until well browned. Stir in the chilli flakes, tomato purée, cumin, raisins, hard-boiled eggs and olives. Simmer together for 5 minutes. Season and leave to cool.

Roll out the dough to a thickness of about 3 mm (⅛ in). Cut around a saucer to make 24 circles, 12 cm (4¾ in) in diameter. Divide the filling between the dough circles and moisten the edges with the remaining beaten egg. Fold over to enclose the filling, then press down well and seal with the prongs of a fork to create a pretty edge.

Fry in a shallow frying pan with a little vegetable oil for 2–3 minutes on each side, until golden. Serve warm.

6

fish
main
courses

salt cod fishcakes with lime and garlic mayonnaise ■ amazonian **monkfish kebabs** ■ grilled chilli **king prawns** ■ admired avocado **salsa pasta** ■ crusted chilli **sprat fish fans** ■ **mussels** in coconut cream and asian spices ■ easy-peasy **prawn paella** ■ hua hin beach **red snapper** ■ **spiced citrus prawns** with herbs and linguine pasta ■ **grilled tuna** with green lentil salad ■ **baked bream** with shrimp and crab, and spicy tomato sauce ■ **fresh braii tuna** and sweet potato chips ■ **lime-skewered cod** with tomato and caper salsa ■ crab and coconut **fishcakes** ■ audacious **anchovy and aubergine tagliatelle** ■ **chilli-lemon-splashed fish** ■ **superb mackerel** with chilli and herbs

salt cod fishcakes
with lime and garlic mayonnaise

Once you've tried salt cod, the flavour is forever remembered. Made into fishcakes, it's a new taste sensation.

SERVES 4

1 x 150 G (5 OZ) PIECE SALT COD, SOAKED IN COLD WATER
  FOR 24 HOURS
3-4 TABLESPOONS OLIVE OIL
450 G (1 LB) COLD BOILED POTATOES, ROUGHLY MASHED
½ TEASPOON GROUND CUMIN
LARGE BUNCH OF CHIVES, SNIPPED
1 EGG, BEATEN
A FEW SHAKES OF TABASCO
SALT AND FRESHLY GROUND BLACK PEPPER
1 TEASPOON CUMIN SEEDS

FOR THE LIME AND GARLIC MAYONNAISE:
1 LARGE EGG YOLK, AT ROOM TEMPERATURE
A SQUEEZE OF LIME JUICE
150 ML (5 FL OZ) MIXED SUNFLOWER AND OLIVE OIL
4 GARLIC CLOVES, PEELED AND CRUSHED
SALT

METHOD

Drain the salt cod and cook in a saucepan of boiling water for 3–4 minutes, or brush with a little olive oil and cook under a hot grill for 2–3 minutes on each side, until soft enough to flake the flesh.

Meanwhile, make the garlic mayonnaise. Place the egg in a large bowl with a squeeze of lime juice and whisk until well blended. Gradually beat in the oil to make a smooth, thick mayonnaise. Stir in the garlic and add salt to taste.

Pull the skin off the fish and discard. Flake the fish, discarding any bones, then stir into the mashed potato with the ground cumin, all but 1 tablespoon of the chives, enough beaten egg to bind firmly, and Tabasco. Season lightly.

Shape the mixture into 4 even-sized cakes. Brush lightly with olive oil and sprinkle with the cumin seeds.

Shallow-fry for 2–3 minutes on each side until golden. Serve with a dollop of garlic mayonnaise and a sprinkling of the reserved chives.

amazonian monkfish kebabs

For this recipe, you'll get the best results from monkfish. I've combined the fish here with some English and Oriental flavourings and made some pretty tasty skewers. Always use a good-quality chilli oil that contains shrimp paste so that you get flavour as well as heat.

SERVES 4

8 x 25 CM (10 IN) BAMBOO OR METAL SKEWERS

500 G (1 LB 2 OZ) CUBED MONKFISH

2 TABLESPOONS SOY SAUCE

1 TABLESPOON TOMATO PURÉE

JUICE OF 1 LIME

1 TABLESPOON VINEGAR

1 TABLESPOON CLEAR HONEY

½ TEASPOON FISH SAUCE

½ TEASPOON CHILLI OIL

1 TABLESPOON FRESH CHOPPED CORIANDER

STIR-FRIED UDON NOODLES (PAGE 139), TO SERVE

METHOD

If using bamboo skewers, put them to soak in cold water for 30 minutes.

Thread the monkfish on to the skewers. Mix together the soy sauce, tomato purée, lime juice, vinegar, honey, fish sauce, chilli oil and coriander, then brush over the kebabs.

Cook the skewers under a pre-heated grill or over hot coals for about 6–8 minutes, turning frequently, until the fish is cooked through and a little charred. Serve on a bed of *Stir-fried Udon Noodles*.

grilled chilli king prawns

Everyone loves to have prawns as a special treat, and these ones are truly special. You could use either large raw king prawns that still have their heads on, or the raw, headless tiger prawns that you can now get from most supermarkets, either from the fresh fish counter or the freezer cabinet.

SERVES 6

36 RAW FRESHWATER KING PRAWNS OR 72 HEADLESS RAW
   TIGER PRAWNS

3 TABLESPOONS VEGETABLE OIL

1 TABLESPOON CLEAR HONEY

1 TABLESPOON CHILLI SAUCE

FINELY GRATED ZEST AND JUICE OF ½ LIME

3-4 GARLIC CLOVES, PEELED AND CRUSHED

SALT AND FRESHLY GROUND BLACK PEPPER

6-12 x 25 CM (10 IN) FINE METAL SKEWERS

CARROT SALAD AND LEMON WEDGES, TO SERVE

METHOD

Peel the prawns, leaving the tail section in place. Make a shallow cut along the curved back of each one and lift out the dark, thread-like intestine.

Mix the rest of the ingredients together in a large bowl. Stir the prawns into the mixture and leave them to marinate in the fridge for at least 20 minutes and up to 2 hours.

Thread the prawns on to the skewers. If using king prawns, you will be able to thread 6 prawns on to 1 skewer for each person. If using tiger prawns, you will need to do 2 skewers per person.

Cook the prawns under a hot grill, or barbecue them over medium-hot coals, for about 3–4 minutes, turning them now and then, until they have become firm and opaque. Eat them straight away while they're still hot. Finger licking permitted. I like to serve them with some crunchy carrot salad and wedges of lemon for squeezing over.

admired avocado salsa pasta

Talk about a feast for the eyes. This warm pasta salad is so full of colour, texture and life that it will win gasps of admiration even before the first bite.

SERVES 4

350 G (12 OZ) PASTA BOWS OR SPIRALS

½ SMALL RED ONION, FINELY CHOPPED

1 AVOCADO, SKINNED, STONED AND FINELY DICED

4 TOMATOES, SEEDED AND FINELY DICED

2 TABLESPOONS CHOPPED FRESH CORIANDER

2 TABLESPOONS FRESH LIME JUICE

3 TABLESPOONS OLIVE OIL

SALT AND PEPPER

2 GARLIC CLOVES, PEELED AND CHOPPED

1 RED CHILLI, SEEDED AND THINLY SLICED

175 G (6 OZ) FRESH OR TINNED CRABMEAT

GROUND CAYENNE PEPPER, TO GARNISH

METHOD

Cook the pasta in a large pan of salted water, according to packet instructions.

Meanwhile, make the avocado salsa. Mix together the red onion, avocado, tomatoes, coriander, lime juice and 1 tablespoon of the olive oil. Season the salsa with salt and pepper and set aside.

Heat the remaining oil in a small pan and cook the garlic and chilli for 30 seconds. Add the crabmeat to the pan and heat through briefly.

Drain the pasta and return to the pan, then stir in the warmed crabmeat mixture. Stir in half of the avocado salsa and divide between four warmed serving plates. Spoon over the remaining avocado salsa and sprinkle with a little ground cayenne pepper to garnish.

crusted chilli sprat fish fans

Good supermarkets now stock sprats and, of course, your local fishmonger will always get them for you if they're not in stock already.

SERVES 4

16 SPRATS, CLEANED

SALT AND FRESHLY GROUND BLACK PEPPER

LEMON OR LIME WEDGES, TO SERVE

FOR THE FILLING:

2 TABLESPOONS CHOPPED FRESH PARSLEY

2 GARLIC CLOVES, PEELED AND CRUSHED

GRATED ZEST OF 1 LIME

FOR THE COATING:

4 TABLESPOONS PLAIN FLOUR

2 TEASPOONS CAYENNE PEPPER

2 TABLESPOONS OLIVE OIL

METHOD

Make the filling by mixing together the parsley, garlic and lime zest.

Open each fish and season the cavity, then sprinkle in a little of the parsley mixture.

Place 4 fish in a row, then angle them so that the tails are on top of each other with the fish splayed out like a fan. Tie a piece of string around the tails to hold the fish in position. Repeat to make 4 fish fans.

Place the flour, cayenne and some salt and pepper in a large shallow dish. Brush the fish fans with olive oil, then dust them with the seasoned flour. Cook in a large frying pan or over hot coals for 3–4 minutes on each side until golden brown and cooked through.

mussels in coconut cream
and asian spices

I love to serve these with freshly cooked chips or even some barbecued potato wedges for dipping in the yummy coconut sauce. I use my old roasting tin for this, but you can use any large, sturdy pan.

SERVES 2

1 TABLESPOON SUNFLOWER OIL

1 TEASPOON THAI GREEN CURRY PASTE

1 GARLIC CLOVE, PEELED AND FINELY CHOPPED

1 TABLESPOON FINELY CHOPPED FRESH ROOT GINGER

½ TEASPOON GROUND TURMERIC

1 x 150 ML (5 FL OZ) CARTON COCONUT CREAM

2 KAFFIR LIME LEAVES, SHREDDED (OPTIONAL)

1 LEMONGRASS STALK, FINELY CHOPPED

1 KG (2¼ LB) FRESH MUSSELS

2 TEASPOONS FISH SAUCE

1 TEASPOON CASTER SUGAR

JUICE OF 1 LIME

A HANDFUL OF FRESH BASIL LEAVES, ROUGHLY TORN

METHOD

Place a roasting tin on the stove top or directly on to hot coals and add the oil. Cook the curry paste, garlic and ginger for 1–2 minutes. Add the turmeric, coconut cream, lime leaves (if using) and lemongrass and bring to the boil.

Add the mussels and cook for 7 minutes or so, shaking the pan occasionally, until the mussel shells open (discard any that remain closed).

Sprinkle over the fish sauce, caster sugar and lime juice and stir well to distribute. Remove from the heat and transfer to serving bowls. Scatter over the basil leaves and serve hot.

easy-peasy prawn paella

A one-pot classic dish that is always satisfying, yet it takes less than half an hour from start to finish. I've used smoked ham to give it a lovely distinctive flavour.

SERVES 4

2 TABLESPOONS VEGETABLE OIL

1 ONION, SLICED

1 RED PEPPER, SEEDED AND DICED

1 GARLIC CLOVE, PEELED AND CRUSHED

200 G (7 OZ) LONG-GRAIN RICE

175 G (6 OZ) SMOKED HAM, ROUGHLY DICED

900 ML (1½ PINTS) CHICKEN OR VEGETABLE STOCK

½ TEASPOON PAPRIKA

½ TEASPOON TURMERIC

175 G (6 OZ) LARGE PRAWNS, THAWED IF FROZEN

100 G (4 OZ) FROZEN PEAS

SALT AND FRESHLY GROUND BLACK PEPPER

METHOD

Heat the oil in a large frying pan and cook the onion for 3–4 minutes until softened and golden. Add the red pepper, garlic and rice and stir-fry for 1 minute. Add the ham, stock, paprika and turmeric, bring to the boil and simmer for 12 minutes.

Stir in the prawns and peas and cook for a further 3–4 minutes until the rice and vegetables are tender. Season to taste, then divide between 4 plates and serve immediately. Ooh, how about a glass of Rioja?

hua hin beach red snapper

I first cooked this at Hua Hin, Thailand, on the beach of the head-shaped stones to the delight of many local fishermen and their families. It's an experience they, and I, will never forget. Just wait 'til you taste it. Substitute red snapper with grey snapper, salmon, trout or sea bass if you wish.

SERVES 4

COCKTAIL STICKS

4 x 350 G (12 OZ) RED SNAPPER

BANANA LEAVES OR EXTRA THICK FOIL

4 HEAPED TABLESPOONS THAI RED CURRY PASTE

4 HEAPED TABLESPOONS COCONUT MILK POWDER

4 LIMES

4 GARLIC CLOVES, PEELED

4 SPRING ONIONS

METHOD

Soak the cocktail sticks in cold water for 30 minutes.

Clean the snapper, remove the scales by scraping them from the tail end to the head with a large blunt knife and then cut off the fins. Cut several deep slashes into both sides of each fish and place them in the centre of a banana leaf or a large square of foil.

Mix the red curry paste and coconut milk powder together into a thick paste and rub it into the fish, making sure that some of it goes right down into the slashes.

Cut two of the limes into thin slices. Push one piece into each of the slashes along one side of each fish.

Thinly slice the garlic and spring onions and sprinkle over the top of each fish. Wrap the leaves or foil over the fish to make well-sealed parcels, secure with cocktail sticks and bake in an oven preheated to 200°C/400°F/gas mark 6 or over medium-hot coals for 15–20 minutes, turning occasionally, until the snappers are completely cooked through and tender.

Remove the cocktail sticks and serve each fish straight from its leaf or foil container. Allow each person to open their own parcel, as the aroma is sensational.

spiced citrus prawns
with herbs and linguine pasta

This dish can be prepared in 20 minutes and makes a perfect light lunch or supper. It proved to be one of the most popular dishes I ever prepared on the *Good Morning* show. You can use spaghetti if you can't get linguine.

SERVES 2-3

450 G (1 LB) LINGUINE PASTA

SALT

6 TABLESPOONS OLIVE OIL

½ SMALL ONION, FINELY CHOPPED

1 GARLIC CLOVE, PEELED AND CRUSHED

1 TABLESPOON CURRY PASTE

1 TABLESPOON CHOPPED FRESH CORIANDER

1 TABLESPOON CHOPPED FRESH MINT

1 TABLESPOON CHOPPED FRESH PARSLEY

225 G (8 OZ) PEELED PRAWNS

ZEST AND JUICE OF 1 LEMON

FRESHLY GROUND BLACK PEPPER

CRUSTY FRENCH BREAD, TO SERVE

METHOD

Cook the pasta in a large pan of salted water, according to packet instructions. When *al dente*, remove from the heat and drain.

Heat the olive oil in a large frying pan or wok, add the onion and garlic and fry without allowing them to colour. Over a medium heat, stir in the curry paste, herbs, peeled prawns, zest and juice of the lemon, and 2–3 tablespoons of water (from the pasta pan, if you like).

Lightly season with salt and pepper, add the drained pasta and toss or mix well together. Serve with some crusty French bread and cold beer or wine.

grilled tuna with green lentil salad

Tuna is the fillet steak of the fish world. It should be cooked lightly, as overcooking will dry it out. You can even eat it slightly underdone. Don't be put off – remember sushi, the Japanese raw fish delicacy. Swordfish and salmon can also be used. If you prefer to use dried lentils, cook them in chicken stock with a few vegetables (e.g. carrots, celery, onion, garlic) and a bay leaf.

SERVES 2

1 x 450 G (1 LB) TIN GREEN LENTILS

2 PLUM TOMATOES, FINELY CHOPPED

50 G (2 OZ) DICED MIXED PEPPERS (RED, GREEN OR YELLOW)

1 CHILLI, FINELY CHOPPED

1 SPRING ONION, TRIMMED AND FINELY CHOPPED

2 TABLESPOONS SOY SAUCE

1 TABLESPOON WHITE WINE VINEGAR

3 TABLESPOONS OLIVE OIL

1 TABLESPOON MIXED CHOPPED FRESH HERBS (E.G. CORIANDER, BASIL AND PARSLEY)

SALT AND FRESHLY GROUND BLACK PEPPER

2 x 175 G (6 OZ) FRESH TUNA FISH STEAKS

A SPRIG OF FRESH CORIANDER, TO GARNISH

METHOD

Put the lentils into a saucepan and warm slightly. Remove from the heat and drain. (If using dried lentils, after cooking drain and remove the vegetables and bay leaf.) Place in a large bowl and then add the chopped tomatoes, peppers, chilli and spring onion. Now add the soy sauce, vinegar, 2 tablespoons of the olive oil, and the fresh herbs. Season, mix well and set aside.

Heat a chargrill pan until hot. Season the tuna and brush with the remaining olive oil. Grill for 2–3 minutes on each side, depending on the thickness of the steaks. Place a mound of lentil salad in the middle of a plate, carve the tuna steak at an angle and arrange on top of the salad with a sprig of fresh coriander.

baked bream with shrimp and crab, and spicy tomato sauce

Another one of those dishes that cooks equally well in the oven or on the barbecue. If you can't get sea bream, use any large fish suitable for stuffing, such as pollack, sea bass or cod. Ask your fishmonger to bone out the fish from the belly so that only one side is open for stuffing.

SERVES 4-6

OIL, FOR BRUSHING
1.5-1.75 KG (3-4 LB) WHOLE FISH, BONED AND CLEANED

FOR THE STUFFING:
1 ONION, PEELED AND FINELY CHOPPED
1 RED PEPPER, SEEDED AND CHOPPED
1 GARLIC CLOVE, PEELED AND CRUSHED
2.5 CM (1 IN) FRESH ROOT GINGER, PEELED AND CHOPPED
175 G (6 OZ) COOKED PEELED PRAWNS
175 G (6 OZ) WHITE CRABMEAT (FRESH OR TINNED)
75 G (3 OZ) WHITE BREADCRUMBS
1 TABLESPOON CHOPPED FRESH CORIANDER
2 GLASSES DRY WHITE WINE
½ TEASPOON PERI PERI SEASONING OR CAYENNE PEPPER
3 TABLESPOONS OLIVE OIL
SALT AND FRESHLY GROUND BLACK PEPPER
LEMON WEDGES, TO GARNISH

FOR THE SPICY TOMATO SAUCE:
2 TABLESPOONS OLIVE OIL
1 ONION, PEELED AND FINELY CHOPPED
1 RED CHILLI, SEEDED AND CHOPPED
½ GREEN PEPPER, SEEDED AND FINELY DICED
2 CELERY STICKS, TRIMMED AND FINELY DICED
1 TABLESPOON CHOPPED FRESH MIXED HERBS
   (E.G. PARSLEY AND BASIL)
A SPLASH OF DRY WHITE WINE
1 x 400 G (14 OZ) TIN CHOPPED TOMATOES
1 TABLESPOON TOMATO PURÉE

METHOD

Pre-heat the oven (if not using the barbecue) to 220°C/425°F/gas mark 7.

Take two large sheets of foil, place one on top of the other, brush with oil and lay your prepared fish on top. Mix together the stuffing ingredients, using 2 tablespoons of the olive oil, along with enough wine to bind the stuffing together (make sure it's not too soggy). Use your hands to fill the inside of the fish with the stuffing. Brush the outside of the fish with the remaining oil, then fold the foil loosely, tucking in the top and ends to form a pillow. This allows steam to circulate around the fish. Put on a baking sheet in the oven or on to a hot barbecue for 35–40 minutes.

Whilst cooking the fish, make the tomato sauce. Heat the oil in a pan, add the onion and fry for 1 minute. Then add the chilli, pepper and celery, fry for another 2 minutes and add the herbs, white wine, tomatoes and tomato purée. Slowly bring to the boil, then cover and simmer for 10–12 minutes. Taste and adjust the seasoning. Place the fish on an oval dish and present inside the foil with the sauce on the side. Garnish with lemon wedges.

fresh braii tuna
and sweet potato chips

Most of the tuna caught off the South African coast is exported, and nobody knows the reason why. Well, they didn't until they tasted my heavenly fish and chips. The fishermen lapped it up, and I have a feeling that the odd one or two will now end up on the barbie or, as they say in South Africa, the braii.

SERVES 4

4 x 275 G (10 OZ) RED-SKINNED SWEET POTATOES, CUT INTO CHUNKY WEDGES

4 GARLIC CLOVES, PEELED

1 TEASPOON COARSE SEA SALT

2 LONG RED FINGER CHILLIES

100 G (4 OZ) MAYONNAISE

1 HEAPED TABLESPOON CHOPPED FRESH FLATLEAF PARSLEY

2 TABLESPOONS OLIVE OIL

2 TABLESPOONS MIXED PEPPERCORNS (BLACK, WHITE, PINK AND GREEN)

4 x 175 G (6 OZ) TUNA STEAKS

METHOD

Drop the wedges of sweet potato into a pan of lightly salted water and cook for about 10 minutes until just tender.

Meanwhile, put the garlic cloves on a board and flatten them with the blade of a large knife. Sprinkle over the salt and continue to crush them with the blade of the knife until they form a smooth paste.

Cut the chillies in half, remove the seeds and thinly slice. Stir into the mayonnaise with the garlic and chopped parsley and set to one side.

Drain the sweet potatoes and toss them in the oil until well coated and season with a little salt. Place them in a large roasting tin and roast for 15–20 minutes. Alternatively, arrange them on a meshed wire rack and barbecue over medium-hot coals for 6–8 minutes, turning every now and then, until lightly golden.

Crush the peppercorns in a pestle and mortar or in a coffee mug using the end of a rolling pin. Press them firmly on to the outside of each tuna steak. Cook the steaks in a heated chargill pan over a high heat or on the barbie for about 2 minutes on each side for a medium-rare steak.

Pile the chips into the centre of 4 plates and place a tuna steak on top. Add a good dollop of the red chilli mayonnaise to each plate and serve the rest separately in a small bowl. Get dunkin'.

lime-skewered cod
with tomato and caper salsa

This dish presents beautifully, and is ideal for a quick supper. My lively lime marinade really firms up the fish nicely for grilling. To add an extra kick to your salsa, simply add one small, fresh chilli, seeded and chopped.

SERVES 3

6 x 25 CM (10 IN) METAL OR BAMBOO SKEWERS

450 G (1 LB) SKINNED THICK COD FILLETS, CUBED

GRATED ZEST OF 1 LIME

JUICE OF 2 LIMES

3 TABLESPOONS OLIVE OIL

SALT AND FRESHLY GROUND BLACK PEPPER

3 TOMATOES, SEEDED AND CHOPPED

1 SMALL RED ONION, FINELY CHOPPED

1 TABLESPOON CHOPPED FRESH PARSLEY OR CORIANDER

1 TABLESPOON DRAINED CAPERS

1 COURGETTE, DIAGONALLY SLICED

225 G (8 OZ) TAGLIATELLE

METHOD

If using bamboo skewers, put them to soak in cold water for 30 minutes to prevent them burning.

Mix together the cubed cod, lime zest, half the lime juice and 1 tablespoon of the oil. Season with salt and pepper and set aside to marinate for 5 minutes.

Mix the tomato flesh, onion, 1 tablespoon of the oil, the parsley or coriander, capers and the remaining lime juice.

Preheat the grill to high. Thread the cod cubes and courgette slices on to six skewers, season and grill for 8–10 minutes, turning once, until tender and golden.

Meanwhile, cook the tagliatelle in a large pan of salted water, according to packet instructions. Drain, then toss with the remaining oil. Fork some tagliatelle into the centre of each plate, top with two kebabs and spoon over some salsa.

crab and coconut fishcakes

These fishcakes are quite soft so they require careful handling when shaping and turning over during cooking, They firm up when cooked for a truly pleasurable treat... Enjoy!

SERVES 4

150 G (5 OZ) FIRM WHITE FISH, SUCH AS COD, HADDOCK OR
   COLEY, SKINNED AND BONED
1 TABLESPOON THAI FISH SAUCE
1 TABLESPOON OYSTER SAUCE
2 GARLIC CLOVES, PEELED AND CRUSHED
SALT AND FRESHLY GROUND WHITE PEPPER
350 G (12 OZ) WHITE CRABMEAT (FRESH OR TINNED), SQUEEZED
   TO REMOVE ANY EXCESS MOISTURE
1 MEDIUM EGG, BEATEN
25 G (1 OZ) UNSWEETENED DESICCATED COCONUT
1 RED FINGER CHILLI, SEEDED AND THINLY SLICED
4 SPRING ONIONS, TRIMMED AND THINLY SLICED
3 TABLESPOONS CHOPPED FRESH CORIANDER
1-2 TABLESPOONS SUNFLOWER OIL, FOR FRYING
SWEET CHILLI SAUCE (PAGE 141), TO SERVE

METHOD

Cut the fish into chunks and check that no bones have been left behind. Place the fish into a food processor with the Thai fish sauce, oyster sauce, garlic and some salt and pepper and process for a few seconds until it has formed a rough paste.

Add the crabmeat and the egg and process once more for just a few seconds until well blended.

Scrape the mixture into a bowl and mix in the coconut, chilli, spring onions and coriander.

Shape the mixture into 8 x 7.5 cm (3 in) patties. Fry in a heated shallow frying pan with 1–2 tablespoons of oil over a medium heat for about 3–4 minutes on each side, until golden brown. Serve immediately with my *Sweet Chilli Sauce* for dipping or drizzling.

audacious anchovy and
aubergine tagliatelle

This is certainly one for all those daring anchovy lovers. Each mouthful ignites your taste buds with a bold, tantalizing experience. Vegetarians who occasionally eat fish might well like this dish. Use the tinned, salted anchovies in oil.

SERVES 4

1 LARGE AUBERGINE, CUT INTO 1 CM (½ IN) CUBES

4 TABLESPOONS OLIVE OIL

½ TEASPOON CHILLI FLAKES (OPTIONAL BUT NICE) OR CAYENNE PEPPER

400 G (14 OZ) DRIED TAGLIATELLE

1 ONION, SLICED

2 GARLIC CLOVES, PEELED AND CRUSHED

3–4 PLUM TOMATOES, SEEDED AND CUT INTO STRIPS

6–8 ANCHOVY FILLETS, DRAINED AND CHOPPED

6–8 FRESH BASIL LEAVES TORN INTO SMALL PIECES

SALT AND FRESHLY GROUND BLACK PEPPER

FRESHLY GRATED PARMESAN

METHOD

Pre-heat oven to 220°C/425°F/gas mark 7.

Spread the diced aubergine out on to a baking sheet. Drizzle over a little olive oil and sprinkle with chilli flakes or dust lightly with cayenne pepper. Pop into the hot oven for 10 minutes until golden.

Cook the pasta in a large pan of salted water, according to packet instructions. Heat the remaining oil and fry the onions for 1–2 minutes. Add the garlic, tomatoes and anchovy and cook over a gentle heat for 2–3 minutes. Add the roasted aubergine and torn basil pieces and give it a really good stir.

Drain the pasta, then return to the saucepan and throw in the aubergine mixture. Season and serve with grated Parmesan and freshly ground black pepper.

chilli-lemon-splashed fish

It's fluffy, it's puffy, it's pulling in the crowds, I am, of course, referring to couscous. It's a great store cupboard standby as it's pre-cooked and is ready to serve in just a couple of minutes. Go on, give it a try, it'll give mealtimes a fluffy feel.

SERVES 4

1 LEMON

4 x 120 G (4¼ OZ) COD OR HADDOCK FILLETS, UNSKINNED

3 TABLESPOONS OLIVE OIL, PLUS EXTRA FOR BRUSHING

SALT AND FRESHLY GROUND BLACK PEPPER

2 GARLIC CLOVES, PEELED AND FINELY CHOPPED

1 RED PEPPER, SEEDED AND FINELY DICED

175 G (6 OZ) COUSCOUS

300 ML (10 FL OZ) HOT VEGETABLE STOCK

2 TOMATOES, FINELY DICED

4 SALAD ONIONS, FINELY CHOPPED

2 TABLESPOONS CHOPPED FRESH CORIANDER OR PARSLEY

¼ TEASPOON CHILLI POWDER

METHOD

Pre-heat the grill to high.

Cut four slices from the lemon and squeeze the juice from the remainder into a small bowl. Place the fish fillets on the grill pan, skin side up, and lay the lemon slices on top. Brush with a little olive oil and season with salt and pepper. Grill for 6–8 minutes, without turning, until cooked and golden.

Meanwhile, heat 1 tablespoon of the olive oil in a large pan and cook the garlic and pepper for 4–5 minutes until softened. Stir in the couscous, hot stock, tomatoes, salad onions and coriander or parsley. Season to taste, cover and remove from the heat.

Mix the lemon juice with the remaining 2 tablespoons of oil and the chilli powder. Fork up the couscous until fluffy, then spoon on to serving plates, place the fish on top and drizzle over the chilli dressing.

superb mackerel with chilli and herbs

Mackerel is a firm favourite of mine. Packed full of vitamins A and D, it's excellent value for money and available all year round. For a healthy diet, oily fish should be eaten at least once a week. Use 1–2 chillies, depending on their size and how hot you like it.

SERVES 4

4 x 275 G (10 OZ) WHOLE MACKEREL, GUTTED AND CLEANED

3 TABLESPOONS FRESH MIXED HERBS (E.G. CHIVES, CHERVIL, DILL, PARSLEY AND TARRAGON), CHOPPED

1-2 RED CHILLIES, SEEDED AND FINELY CHOPPED

1 TABLESPOON SESAME OIL

2 TABLESPOONS OLIVE OIL

2 TABLESPOONS SOY SAUCE

FRESHLY GROUND BLACK PEPPER

OIL, FOR FRYING

RICE AND GREEN SALAD, TO SERVE

METHOD

Make three 5 mm (¼ in) deep slashes across one side of each fish. Reserve 1 tablespoon of the herbs and smear the rest inside the fish. Mix together the reserved herbs, chilli, sesame and olive oils, soy sauce and pepper. Spoon over the fish, working it into the grooves. Place in a dish and cover and chill for 2 hours.

Heat the oil in a large frying pan. Cook the fish on the uncut side for 4 minutes. Place under a medium grill, cut-side up, for 4–6 minutes until crisp and cooked through. Serve with rice and a green salad.

7

vegetarian main courses

marinated goats' cheese in vine leaf parcels ■ **pecorino pasta** with olives and chilli broccoli ■ **aubergine** stuffed with asian vegetables ■ roll up, roll up **spinach and stilton roulade** ■ corta spini-**chilli pasta** ■ tingling **thai-spiced vegetables** with couscous ■ baked potato, pepper and onion **frittata** ■ plantain, pumpkin and **chick pea curry** ■ spicy **veggie beanburgers** ■ speedy **cornzales cheesy parcels** ■ charred smoked **tofu satay** ■ spicy **sweet potato and apple bake** ■ greek **halloumi and pitta salad** with caper dressing ■ mighty mexican **tortilla cheesecake** ■ avocado cone quesadillas

marinated goats' cheese
in vine leaf parcels

This dish needs to be made with those small, individual goats' cheeses with a rind. Crotin de Chavignol is a name to look out for.

The vine leaves provide a protective coating, hold in all the marinade flavours and impart a lemony flavour to the cooked cheese. If you are lucky enough to be able to get hold of fresh vine leaves then great, but otherwise use vine leaves that have been vacuum-packed in brine, which are available from most delicatessens and larger supermarkets.

This dish is quite rich (the quantities below will make two small parcels per person), but double the quantities if you don't think there's going to be enough for a main course.

SERVES 4

COCKTAIL STICKS

8 LARGE OR 16 SMALLER VINE LEAVES

4 x 100 G (4 OZ) INDIVIDUAL GOATS' CHEESES

4 TABLESPOONS OLIVE OIL

2 RED FINGER CHILLIES, SEEDED AND FINELY CHOPPED

2 TEASPOONS CHOPPED FRESH OREGANO

12 FRESH BASIL LEAVES, FINELY SHREDDED

1 GARLIC CLOVE, PEELED AND FINELY CHOPPED

½ TEASPOON BLACK PEPPERCORNS, COARSELY CRUSHED

COARSE SEA SALT

8 SMALL FRESH BAY LEAVES

1 LOAF OF CIABATTA, TO SERVE

METHOD

Put the cocktail sticks to soak in cold water for 30 minutes.

If you are using fresh vine leaves, remove the tough part of the stem, drop them into a pan of lightly salted water and cook for about 4 minutes. Drain and refresh under cold water. If you are using preserved vine leaves, soak them in hot water, rinse in cold water and drain. Cut the goats' cheeses in half horizontally into 2 smaller discs.

Mix the olive oil with the chopped chilli, oregano, basil, garlic, crushed pepper and a little salt. Place a vine leaf on a plate (overlap 2 if they're quite small) and put a bay leaf and a little of the marinade into the centre.

Place a disc of goats' cheese on top, rind-side down, and then spoon over a bit more of the marinade. Fold over the sides of the leaves and secure in place with one or more cocktail sticks. Repeat 3 more times.

Place the parcels in a shallow dish, pour over any oil left on the plate and set aside for 1 hour.

Brush the outside of the vine leaf parcels with a little more olive oil if necessary and barbecue over medium-hot coals for about 2½ minutes on each side. Lift the parcels on to plates, remove the cocktail sticks and fold back the leaves. Serve with the ciabatta.

pecorino pasta
with olives and chilli broccoli

Pecorino is like Parmesan, but with a sharper taste that goes exceptionally well with dishes that have quite a strong flavour – like this one perhaps… Don't let the Pecorino put you off (use Parmesan if you have to) but, if you feel in the mood, buy it and try it!

SERVES 2-3

450 G (1 LB) FRESH OR DRIED FUSILLI PASTA

250 G (9 OZ) BROCCOLI, CUT INTO LITTLE FLORETS

6 TABLESPOONS OLIVE OIL

2-3 GARLIC CLOVES, PEELED AND CRUSHED

½ TABLESPOON DRIED CHILLI FLAKES OR 1 TABLESPOON
  CHOPPED CHIVES

6 SUN-DRIED OR SUNBLUSH TOMATOES, CUT INTO STRIPS

4 BLACK OLIVES, SLICED

SALT AND FRESHLY GROUND BLACK PEPPER

FRESHLY GRATED PECORINO

METHOD

Cook the pasta in a large pan of salted water, according to packet instructions. When *al dente*, remove from the heat and drain.

Blanch the broccoli florets in boiling water for 1 minute and drain. (I steam mine in the microwave oven for about 40 seconds.)

Heat the olive oil in a large frying pan or wok. Add the garlic and chilli or chives and fry on a medium to high heat for 20 seconds. Then add the sun-dried tomatoes, olives and broccoli. Stir-fry for 30 seconds. Increase the heat, throw in the pasta, toss, season and serve with grated Pecorino. A few bottles of Pils lager add a little something to this light, spicy supper.

aubergine stuffed with asian vegetables

It looks good, it tastes great and it's ideal for that special barbecue date. Having said that, you can cook it all in your chargrill pan in your nice and cosy kitchen.

SERVES 4

16 x 12 CM (4¾ IN) BAMBOO SKEWERS

2 LARGE AUBERGINES

SUNFLOWER OIL, FOR BRUSHING

SALT AND FRESHLY GROUND BLACK PEPPER

50 G (2 OZ) GLASS NOODLES, OR OTHER THIN RICE NOODLES

1 LARGE CARROT, CUT INTO MATCHSTICKS

50 G (2 OZ) BEANSPROUTS

2 CM (¾ IN) PIECE FRESH ROOT GINGER, FINELY CHOPPED

A HANDFUL OF FRESH CORIANDER LEAVES

1 TABLESPOON TOASTED SESAME SEEDS

1 TABLESPOON HOISIN SAUCE

1 TABLESPOON SOY SAUCE

BOILED RICE AND SOY SAUCE, TO SERVE

METHOD

Put the skewers to soak in cold water for 30 minutes.

Diagonally cut the aubergine into 16 oval slices, 1 cm (½ in) thick.

Pre-heat a large ridged chargrill pan. Brush the aubergine slices with oil and cook on the chargrill pan or on a barbecue rack over medium-hot coals for 1–2 minutes on each side, until charred.

Meanwhile, place the noodles in a bowl and cover with boiling water. Set aside for 2–3 minutes, or according to the packet instructions, then drain.

Mix together the carrot, beansprouts, ginger, coriander leaves, sesame seeds, hoisin sauce, soy sauce and drained noodles.

Place 8 slices of the aubergine, cooked side uppermost, on a flat surface and spoon the noodle mixture into the centre of each. Top with the remaining aubergine slices, ensuring that the uncooked surface is on the outside.

Use the skewers to pin each aubergine sandwich closed along the long edges, to enclose the filling. Brush with a little more oil and cook for 2–3 minutes on each side until the aubergine is cooked and golden. Serve with boiled rice and extra soy sauce.

roll up, roll up
spinach and stilton roulade

This looks so attractive yet it is easy to make once you've cracked the method. And once you've made this version, you'll find it works with all kinds of fillings, such as cream cheese with smoked fish, horseradish and herbs, or cream cheese with peppers, pine nuts, tomatoes and olives.

SERVES 4

275 G (10 OZ) SPINACH, BLANCHED AND WELL DRAINED

SALT AND FRESHLY GROUND BLACK PEPPER

PINCH OF NUTMEG

3 EGGS, SEPARATED

225 G (8 OZ) FULL-FAT SOFT CHEESE

25 G (1 OZ) FRESHLY GRATED PARMESAN

SPRIGS OF WATERCRESS AND QUARTERED ORANGES, TO GARNISH

FOR THE FILLING:

2 TABLESPOONS CRÈME FRAÎCHE OR NATURAL YOGHURT

3 SPRING ONIONS, TRIMMED AND FINELY SLICED

1 RED CHILLI, SEEDED AND FINELY CHOPPED (OPTIONAL)

50 G (2 OZ) WALNUTS, ROUGHLY CHOPPED

75 G (3 OZ) STILTON CHEESE, CRUMBLED

METHOD

Pre-heat the oven to 190°C/375°F/gas mark 5. Butter a Swiss roll tin 30 x 23 cm (12 x 9 in) and line with greaseproof paper or baking parchment. (If using greaseproof paper, brush with melted butter.) Season the spinach with salt and pepper, and add a pinch of nutmeg. Beat the egg yolks with the cream cheese, season, then stir in the spinach. Whisk the whites until stiff but still soft, then gradually fold into the spinach mixture. Spoon into the prepared tray and bake in the oven for about 12–15 minutes: it should be firm but spongy to the touch.

Lay a piece of greaseproof paper on a flat surface, sprinkle with the Parmesan and turn the roulade out on top of it. Cool slightly (I put a cold damp cloth on top), then peel off the paper and roll up with the new greaseproof paper inside to stop the roulade sticking together.

Mix the filling ingredients together until fairly smooth. Unroll the roulade, carefully remove the paper and spread with the filling. Trim the edges with a sharp knife and roll up again with the filling. Garnish with watercress and orange quarters.

corta spini-chilli pasta

If you like it hot, hot, hot like I sometimes do, use a full teaspoon of chilli – if you prefer a milder flavour, simply halve that amount. Tube pasta like caserecce or rigatoni is best, as the little pockets get filled with the succulent sauce of stringy cheese.

SERVES 4

1 SMALL AUBERGINE, CUT LENGTHWAYS INTO 1 CM (½ IN) SLICES

2-3 TABLESPOONS OLIVE OIL

1 ONION, CHOPPED

2 GARLIC CLOVES, PEELED AND CHOPPED

400 G (14 OZ) CAN CHOPPED TOMATOES

1 TEASPOON DRIED CHILLI FLAKES

350 G (12 OZ) PASTA SHAPES, SUCH AS RIGATONI OR CASERECCE

100 G (4 OZ) FROZEN LEAF SPINACH OR 200 G (7 OZ) FRESH LEAF SPINACH, TRIMMED

100 G (4 OZ) CHEDDAR OR GRUYÈRE, GRATED

SALT AND PEPPER

METHOD

Pre-heat the grill to hot. Lightly brush the aubergine with oil and grill for 2–3 minutes on each side until golden brown. Meanwhile, heat 1 tablespoon of the oil in a pan and cook the onion and garlic for 3–4 minutes until golden. Stir in the tomatoes and chilli flakes, bring to the boil and simmer for 4–5 minutes. Cut the grilled aubergine slices into strips, add to the tomato sauce and cook for a further 4–5 minutes. Season to taste.

Cook the pasta according to packet instructions, adding the frozen spinach for the last 3 minutes. Drain well and return to the pan. If using fresh spinach, remove the pasta from the heat once cooked, stir in the trimmed spinach, then drain.

Stir in the tomato sauce and half the cheese. Transfer to serving plates and scatter over the remaining cheese.

tingling thai-spiced vegetables
with couscous

Get those taste buds tingling with this trendy Thai delight. Simply toss those veggies in a pan and stir in the heavenly sauce. I've served them on a bed of couscous, but you could use rice or pasta.

SERVES 4

2 TABLESPOONS VEGETABLE OIL

1 ONION, SLICED

650 G (1 LB 6 OZ) MIXED VEGETABLES, SUCH AS CARROTS, BROCCOLI,
 CELERY, GREEN BEANS, RUNNER BEANS AND AUBERGINES, CHOPPED

2-3 TEASPOONS THAI RED CURRY PASTE

300 ML (½ PINT) VEGETABLE STOCK

250 G (9 OZ) COUSCOUS

350 ML (12 FL OZ) BOILING WATER OR VEGETABLE STOCK

200 ML (7 FL OZ) CARTON COCONUT CREAM

SALT AND FRESHLY GROUND BLACK PEPPER

50 G (2 OZ) CHOPPED PEANUTS, TO GARNISH

METHOD

Heat the oil in a large pan and cook the sliced onion for 3–4 minutes until golden. If using carrots, add them before the other vegetables and fry for 2 minutes, then add the remaining vegetables and cook for a further 3 minutes. Stir in the curry paste and stock, cover and simmer for 10 minutes until the vegetables are tender but still firm.

Place the couscous in a bowl and pour over the boiling water or stock. Allow to stand for 4–5 minutes, fluffing up with a fork two or three times until the couscous becomes light and crumbly.

Stir the coconut cream into the vegetables, heat through and season. Divide the couscous between four plates, top with spicy vegetables and scatter over the chopped peanuts.

baked potato, pepper and onion frittata

So this is what the Italians do with their eggs. It's superb hot or cold, and you can add any meat, fish or vegetables to it – it will support anything. Try it, it's lovely…

If using a frying pan, make sure it is ovenproof – i.e. no wooden or plastic handles – and make sure it fits in the oven first. Instead of a spring-form tin, a deep metal tart or pie plate will do. You can even cook this frittata on the stove, but baking gives a better finish and taste.

SERVES 4

275 G (10 OZ) POTATOES, PEELED AND CUT INTO 2 CM (1 IN) CUBES
4 TABLESPOONS OLIVE OIL
1 LARGE ONION, PEELED AND FINELY SLICED
½ GREEN PEPPER, SEEDED AND SLICED
½ RED PEPPER, SEEDED AND SLICED
1 GREEN CHILLI, SEEDED AND SLICED
5 LARGE EGGS, BEATEN
250 G (9 OZ) RICOTTA
50 G (2 OZ) FRESHLY GRATED PARMESAN
SALT AND FRESHLY GROUND BLACK PEPPER
GREEN SALAD, TO SERVE

METHOD

Pre-heat the oven to 180°C/350°F/gas mark 4.

Parboil the potatoes in boiling water for 5 minutes and drain. Heat the oil in a frying pan and when hot add the potatoes and fry until golden. Remove with a slotted spoon and drain on kitchen paper. In the same pan, add the onion, peppers and chilli. Cook until the onions are lightly charred, then remove with a slotted spoon and drain on kitchen paper.

Mix the potatoes, onion, peppers and chilli with the beaten eggs, then stir in the Ricotta and Parmesan and season with salt and pepper. Pour into a well-buttered, spring-form tin or an ovenproof buttered frying pan and bake in the oven for 35–40 minutes until the centre is firm and the top golden brown. (You can always brown it a bit more under the grill.) Loosen the frittata around the edge, turn out on to a plate, cool slightly, then cut into wedges and serve hot or cold with salad.

plantain, pumpkin
and chick pea curry

No, you're not going to plant anything except lots of harmonious ingredients into a pot, and when the diners are satisfied you can get them to do some gardening. Plantain is the daddy of bananas, being much larger than the familiar variety. It is never eaten raw. It can be cooked in different ways, depending on its ripeness. Green ones are suitable for plantain chips and stews, yellow for quick frying or curries like this, and yellow-black for desserts. Don't be put off by the blackness – the starch has turned to sugar, darkening the skin.

SERVES 4

4 TABLESPOONS SUNFLOWER OR VEGETABLE OIL

½ TEASPOON WHOLE CUMIN SEEDS

½ TEASPOON RED CHILLI FLAKES

1 ONION, PEELED AND SLICED

2 GARLIC CLOVES, PEELED AND CHOPPED

2.5 CM (1 IN) FRESH ROOT GINGER, PEELED AND GRATED

1 TEASPOON GROUND CORIANDER

½ TEASPOON TURMERIC

5 CM (2 IN) STICK CINNAMON OR ¼ TEASPOON GROUND CINNAMON

450 G (1 LB) PUMPKIN, HALVED, SEEDED AND DICED INTO ABOUT
   2.5 CM (1 IN) PIECES

275 G (10 OZ) PLANTAIN, PEELED AND CUT INTO CUBES

1 x 400 G (14 OZ) TIN CHOPPED TOMATOES

225 G (8 OZ) COOKED CHICK PEAS, DRAINED

2 TABLESPOONS MEDIUM HOT CURRY PASTE

300 ML (½ PINT) VEGETABLE STOCK

1 TABLESPOON CHOPPED FRESH CORIANDER, PLUS EXTRA TO GARNISH

SALT AND FRESHLY GROUND BLACK PEPPER

1 BANANA

1 TABLESPOON LEMON JUICE

BOILED RICE, TO SERVE

METHOD

Heat the oil in a pan. Fry the cumin seeds for 5 seconds, then add the chilli followed by the onion and garlic. Fry for 1 minute, then add the gniger, coriander and remaining spices. Stir and cook for another minute. Add the pumpkin and plantain, mix until all is well coated with the spices and the vegetables begin to turn slightly brown. Add the tomatoes, chick peas, curry paste and vegetable stock, and stir well. Bring to the boil, cover and simmer for 20–25 minutes or until the pumpkin is tender and the sauce is nice and rich.

Stir in the fresh coriander, taste and adjust the seasoning. Peel and slice the banana and toss in the lemon juice. Serve the curry in a bowl with sliced banana on top and a sprinkling of chopped coriander. Accompany with boiled rice.

spicy veggie beanburgers

My beanburgers are nutritious, easy to make and taste great. The kids love to prepare them, and can't wait to eat them. If it's a nice day, why not slap 'em on the barbie?

SERVES 2

1 TABLESPOON VEGETABLE OIL

1 SMALL ONION, FINELY CHOPPED

2 GARLIC CLOVES, PEELED AND FINELY CHOPPED

1 SMALL HOT RED CHILLI, FINELY CHOPPED (OPTIONAL)

100 G (4 OZ) FROZEN CHOPPED SPINACH, THAWED

400 G (14 OZ) TIN CANNELLINI BEANS

50 G (2 OZ) FRESH WHITE BREADCRUMBS

1 TEASPOON GROUND CUMIN

1 TABLESPOON CHOPPED FRESH CORIANDER

SALT AND FRESHLY GROUND BLACK PEPPER

BURGER BUNS, RELISH AND SALAD, TO SERVE

METHOD

Heat the oil in a small saucepan and cook the onion, garlic and chilli (optional) for 5 minutes until softened. Squeeze the excess moisture out of the spinach and place in a large bowl.

Mash the beans well and mix with the spinach, breadcrumbs, cumin and coriander. Add the fried onion mixture and stir together well.

Season to taste and shape into four round burgers. Grill or shallow-fry for a few minutes on each side until crisp and golden. Serve in burger buns with relish and salad.

speedy cornzales cheesy parcels

I made these delicious parcels in the main square, the *Zócalo*, in Oaxaca surrounded by locals and the local police! There was the small problem of needing a filming permit, which had been sent to the wrong address. So yours truly was incredibly speedy before we cheesed off the Bill!

For this recipe I use dried corn husks (available from specialist shops) and canned sweetcorn, but you can always buy whole corn on the cob, save the husks and cook the corn yourself.

SERVES 4

5 DRIED CORN HUSKS

1 x 400 G (14 OZ) TIN CANNELLINI BEANS, RINSED AND DRAINED

200 G (7 OZ) SWEETCORN

4 TABLESPOONS MAYONNAISE

1 BUNCH OF SALAD ONIONS, FINELY CHOPPED

2 GARLIC CLOVES, PEELED AND FINELY CHOPPED

4 TABLESPOONS CHOPPED FRESH PARSLEY

SALT AND FRESHLY GROUND BLACK PEPPER

A FEW DROPS OF TABASCO

150 G (5 OZ) CHEDDAR, GRATED, OR MOZZARELLA, ROUGHLY DICED

SALAD, TO SERVE

METHOD

Soak the corn husks in hot water for 15 minutes until soft and pliable. Meanwhile, mash the cannellini beans and mix with the sweetcorn, mayonnaise, salad onions, garlic and parsley. Add salt, pepper and Tabasco to taste.

Open out 4 of the husks and divide half of the bean mixture between them. Scatter over the cheese, then top with the remaining bean mixture. Fold the edges in to enclose the filling and form a neat, square parcel. Tear the remaining husk into strips 5mm (¼ in) wide and tie these around the centre of each parcel to hold it securely.

Cook under a pre-heated grill or over medium coals for 5–7 minutes on each side until the parcels are warmed through and the husks well browned. Serve with lots of crunchy green salad.

charred smoked tofu satay

I use smoked tofu for this as it has a much firmer texture than the plain variety, and the flavour works very well on a barbecue.

SERVES 2

4 x 25 CM (10 IN) BAMBOO SKEWERS

1 x 300 G (11 OZ) PACK SMOKED TOFU

2 TABLESPOONS SOY SAUCE

1 TABLESPOON CHILLI SAUCE

1 TABLESPOON VEGETABLE OIL

FOR THE SATAY SAUCE:

1 x 150 G (5 OZ) CARTON COCONUT CREAM

4 TABLESPOONS CRUNCHY PEANUT BUTTER

1 TABLESPOON SOY SAUCE

JUICE OF 1 LIME

METHOD

Put the skewers to soak in cold water for 30 minutes.

Cut the tofu into 2 cm (¾ in) cubes. Stir together the soy sauce, chilli sauce and vegetable oil. Add the tofu cubes and set aside to marinate for 1–2 hours.

Place the coconut cream, peanut butter and soy sauce in a small pan and heat gently on the stove or on the edge of the barbecue.

Thread the tofu on to the skewers and cook in a chargrill pan, or barbecue over hot coals, for a minute or so on each side until beginning to brown and crispen a little.

Squeeze the lime juice into the satay sauce, then serve drizzled over the smoked, charred tofu skewers.

spicy sweet potato and apple bake

This delicious recipe is a great vegetarian supper dish, as well as being an excellent accompaniment to spicy pork sausages or roast pork with crispy crackling. Try to use sweet potatoes and apples that are about the same size in diameter.

SERVES 4-6

3 x 225 G (8 OZ) SWEET POTATOES, WASHED

4 x 75 G (3 OZ) FIRM EATING APPLES

75 G (3 OZ) LIGHT MUSCOVADO SUGAR

½ TEASPOON SALT

1½ TEASPOONS GROUND MIXED SPICE

40 G (1½ OZ) BUTTER, PLUS EXTRA FOR GREASING

4 TABLESPOONS WATER

METHOD

Pre-heat the oven to 180°C/350°F/gas mark 4 and butter an ovenproof dish.

Cook the sweet potatoes whole in a pan of boiling, salted water until tender. Drain well and leave to cool. Peel and cut into 5 mm (¼ in) slices. Peel and cut the apples into 5 mm (¼ in) slices and place alternate layers of sweet potato and apple in the buttered dish. Sprinkle each layer with a little sugar, salt and mixed spice. Dot with butter, sprinkle over the water and cover with a lid. Bake for 20 minutes, remove the cover and bake for a further 10 minutes before serving.

greek halloumi and pitta salad
with caper dressing

Halloumi is a delicious Greek cheese that softens but doesn't melt, so it's great for cooking with – but make sure you eat it quickly because it turns slightly rubbery when cold.

SERVES 4

2 x 200 G (7 OZ) PACKETS OF HALLOUMI, CUT INTO SLICES
1 CM (½ IN) THICK
OLIVE OIL, FOR BRUSHING
4 MINI PITTAS, CUT INTO TRIANGULAR FINGERS
1 COS LETTUCE, ROUGHLY SHREDDED
150 G (5 OZ) BABY PLUM TOMATOES, HALVED LENGTHWAYS
50 G (2 OZ) KALAMATA OLIVES

FOR THE DRESSING:
1 TABLESPOON PICKLED CAPERS, RINSED AND ROUGHLY CHOPPED
GRATED ZEST AND JUICE OF 1 LIME
3 TABLESPOONS OLIVE OIL
SALT AND FRESHLY GROUND BLACK PEPPER

METHOD

Begin by making the dressing. Stir together the capers, lime zest and juice, olive oil, a little salt and plenty of black pepper.

Brush the cheese with a little olive oil and cook under a hot grill or in a chargrill pan for 2 minutes on each side until golden. Heat the pitta fingers in the same way for about 30 seconds on each side.

Arrange the lettuce, tomatoes and olives on 4 serving plates. Place the pitta fingers and the cheese on top of the salad and drizzle over the dressing. Eat warm.

mighty mexican tortilla cheesecake

Well, not cheesecake as you know it, but delightful layers of flour tortillas filled with saucy beans, vegetables and grated cheese. Go on... get in on the Mexican feast. A few bottles of Mexican lager help it slip down nicely.

SERVES 4

1 TABLESPOON OLIVE OIL

1 ONION, CHOPPED

½–1 TEASPOON HOT CHILLI POWDER

400 G (14 OZ) TIN CHOPPED TOMATOES WITH HERBS

200 G (7 OZ) FROZEN MIXED VEGETABLES

215 G (7¼ OZ) TIN KIDNEY BEANS, DRAINED

SALT AND FRESHLY GROUND BLACK PEPPER

5 x 25 CM (10 IN) FLOUR TORTILLAS

150 G (5 OZ) MATURE CHEDDAR, GRATED

SHREDDED LETTUCE, SOUR CREAM AND CHOPPED SALAD ONIONS,
   TO SERVE

METHOD

Preheat the oven to 180°C/350°F/gas mark 4.

Heat the oil in a pan and cook the onion for 3–4 minutes until golden. Stir in the chilli powder and tomatoes and cook for 5 minutes, or until slightly thickened. Add the mixed vegetables and heat through for 4 minutes, or until the sauce has thickened. Stir in the beans and heat through, then season.

Place a tortilla on a heatproof plate, spread with a little of the sauce and sprinkle over a handful of cheese. Continue layering the tortillas, sauce and cheese, finishing with a sprinkling of cheese. Place the plate on a baking sheet and warm through in the hot oven for 10 minutes until the cheese has melted. Cut into wedges and serve with shredded lettuce, sour cream and salad onions.

avocado cone quesadillas

When making quesadillas, the tortillas are usually stacked and then cut into wedges, but I prefer to fold them into little cones and serve them individually.

SERVES 4

8 CORN OR FLOUR TORTILLAS

150 G (5 OZ) GRATED CHEESE, SUCH AS MONTEREY JACK,
  CHEDDAR OR WENSLEYDALE

LIME WEDGES, TO GARNISH

FOR THE FILLING:

2 TOMATOES, SEEDED AND DICED

1 LARGE AVOCADO, SKINNED, STONED AND DICED

1 RED ONION, FINELY CHOPPED

JUICE OF ½ LEMON

A FEW DROPS OF TABASCO

SALT AND FRESHLY GROUND BLACK PEPPER

FOR THE TOPPING:

1 x 150 ML (5 FL OZ) CARTON SOUR CREAM

2 TABLESPOONS CHOPPED FRESH CORIANDER

METHOD

Start by making the filling. Stir together the tomatoes, avocado and red onion, then stir in the lemon juice and Tabasco and season to taste.

Prepare the topping by mixing together the sour cream and coriander, then season.

Assemble the quesadillas 2 or 3 at a time. Heat the tortillas under the grill or for about 10 seconds in the microwave, then sprinkle over some cheese followed by the avocado mixture. Quickly fold the tortillas in half and then in half again to make triangular shapes – you need to be speedy to prevent the tortillas crisping up too much before you fold them.

Heat under the grill for a further minute or so on each side until the tortillas are crisp and golden brown and the cheese has melted. Repeat to make 8 quesadillas.

Arrange on plates and top each serving with a dollop of the sour cream mixture. Garnish with a lime wedge and serve warm.

8

vegetables & side orders

grilled corn cob with chilli onion dressing ■ **fiery roasted tomatoes** ■ fire-roasted **red pepper and nectarine salad** ■ **cheese and bubble hotcakes** ■ double-dip **spicy chips** ■ **saffron-scented lemon rice** ■ ranch-style **pit-baked beans** ■ peppy's jamaican **rice and peas** ■ crazy crunchy **crispy coleslaw** ■ flamed **polenta chips** ■ beefsteak **mediterranean tomatoes** ■ **fiery green beans, courgettes and broccoli with lemon thyme** ■ stir-fried **udon noodles**

grilled corn cob
with chilli onion dressing

Sweetcorn are especially good when cooked in their husks on a barbecue. They become really tender because they almost steam in their own juices. The trick is to soak them in cold water for at least 1 hour beforehand so that the husks don't catch fire during cooking. They're flaming lovely!

SERVES 4-6

4-6 EARS OF SWEETCORN IN THEIR HUSKS

175 G (6 OZ) BUTTER

4 TEASPOONS CHILLI OIL (OR MORE IF YOU DARE)

4 GREEN CHILLIES, SEEDED AND VERY FINELY CHOPPED

4 SPRING ONIONS, TRIMMED AND THINLY SLICED

2 TEASPOONS LEMON OR LIME JUICE

SALT AND FRESHLY GROUND BLACK PEPPER

CRUSTY BREAD, TO SERVE

METHOD

Soak the sweetcorn in cold water for at least 1 hour.

Remove the corn from the water, drain away the excess and cook under a medium-hot grill (at least 6 inches away from direct heat), or barbecue over medium-hot coals, for 30 minutes, turning every now and then.

Meanwhile, put the butter into a pan and leave over a low heat until melted. Spoon any scum off the surface and then pour the clear butter into a bowl, leaving behind the milky white liquid.

Just before the sweetcorn is ready, heat the chilli oil in a small clean pan, add the green chillies and fry for 1 minute. Remove from the heat and add the clarified butter, spring onions, lemon or lime juice and plenty of seasoning.

Pull away the browned husks from the outside of the corn, transfer the ears to plates and spoon over the warm dressing. Eat with plenty of crusty bread to mop up all the juices.

fiery roasted tomatoes

To capture all the wonderful flavours of this dish you simply must eat these tomatoes hot or, at least, warm.

SERVES 4-6

500 G (1 LB 2 OZ) POMODORINO OR CHERRY TOMATOES

4 UNPEELED LARGE GARLIC CLOVES

3 RED CHILLIES, SEEDED AND FINELY CHOPPED

2-3 TABLESPOONS OLIVE OIL

SALT AND FRESHLY GROUND BLACK PEPPER

2 TABLESPOONS CHOPPED FRESH PARSLEY, CHIVES OR BASIL

JUICE OF ½ LEMON

METHOD

Preheat oven to 200°C/400°F/gas mark 6. Arrange the tomatoes in a shallow roasting tin. Lightly flatten each unpeeled garlic clove with a heavy knife and tuck these and the chillies between the tomatoes.

Drizzle over the oil, season with salt and pepper and cook in the hot oven or over hot coals for 15–20 minutes, stirring occasionally, until the tomatoes have blistered and slightly softened.

Stir in the herbs and lemon juice, then season to taste.

fire-roasted red pepper
and nectarine salad

Another simple salad that has the beautiful taste of chargrilled pepper, combined with nectarines infused with sweet-sharp balsamic vinegar, olly oil and pepper. There, now isn't that simple!

SERVES 8

8 LARGE RED PEPPERS

4 RIPE BUT FIRM NECTARINES

4 TEASPOONS BALSAMIC VINEGAR

6 TABLESPOONS EXTRA VIRGIN OLIVE OIL

FRESHLY GROUND BLACK PEPPER

METHOD

Cook the peppers under a hot grill or on the barbecue for about 12–15 minutes, turning them regularly, until the skins are completely blackened and blistered.

Drop them into a large plastic bag, seal in some air and leave until cool enough to handle. The captured steam helps to loosen the skins, making them easier to peel.

Cut the peppers in half, remove the skin and seeds and cut the flesh into long thin strips.

Place the peppers in a shallow dish with any juices. Halve the nectarines, remove the stones and thinly slice them into the dish with the peppers. Toss together gently.

Drizzle over the balsamic vinegar and olive oil and season with plenty of black pepper. Serve straight away.

cheese and bubble hotcakes

Perfect for those occasional leftover tatties. I vary the ingredients every time and they always taste great. Add whatever you have to hand: try adding pieces of cooked sausage, bacon or chorizo for a more substantial serving.

Make sure you use floury potatoes, such as King Edward or Maris Piper, as new potatoes aren't starchy enough to hold the cakes together.

SERVES 4

350 G (12 OZ) BOILED OR BAKED POTATOES

150 G (5 OZ) COOKED CABBAGE, BRUSSELS SPROUTS, BROCCOLI
   OR SPINACH, SHREDDED OR CHOPPED

1 GARLIC CLOVE, PEELED AND FINELY CHOPPED

50 G (2 OZ) CHEDDAR, GRATED

A FEW SHAKES OF TABASCO

SALT AND FRESHLY GROUND BLACK PEPPER

2-3 TABLESPOONS OLIVE OIL, FOR FRYING

METHOD

Place the potatoes in a large bowl and mash thoroughly. Stir in the cabbage or other vegetable, garlic, cheese, a good dash of Tabasco and plenty of salt and pepper.

Shape the mixture into 4 even-sized cakes. Cook in a large frying pan with the olive oil for 4–5 minutes on each side until golden.

double-dip spicy chips

To get good, crispy chips with a fluffy centre you need to cook them twice. If you haven't got a deep-fat fryer, heat some oil in a heavy-based saucepan or wok. Only fill it one-third of the way full of oil for safety.

SERVES 4

4 LARGE FLOURY POTATOES, SUCH AS KING EDWARD OR MARIS PIPER

VEGETABLE OIL, FOR DEEP FRYING

CUBES OF BREAD FOR TESTING OIL TEMPERATURE

1–2 TABLESPOONS CAJUN OR CREOLE SEASONING

½ TEASPOON SALT

METHOD

Peel the potatoes and cut into long, thin chips, then wash them thoroughly in cold water. Dry well with kitchen paper.

Pre-heat a deep-fat fryer. Test the temperature with a cube of bread until it turns golden in about 60 seconds: if the fat is too hot, the fries will turn brown before they are cooked. When the oil is ready, cook the chips for 3–4 minutes until pale golden.

Drain the fries on kitchen paper. Raise the oil temperature until a cube of bread browns in 30 seconds. Return fries to the pan and cook for a minute or two until crisp and dark golden. Drain on kitchen paper, then sprinkle with the spicy seasoning and salt. Serve immediately.

saffron-scented lemon rice

A lovely fragrant rice to accompany all sorts of dishes. It really does go with just about all meat, chicken and fish.

SERVES 4

2 TABLESPOONS OLIVE OIL

1 ONION, FINELY CHOPPED

2 GARLIC CLOVES, PEELED AND FINELY CHOPPED

225 G (8 OZ) LONG-GRAIN RICE

750 ML (1¼ PINTS) HOT VEGETABLE STOCK

A PINCH OF SAFFRON STRANDS

A PINCH OF DRIED CHILLI FLAKES

2 TABLESPOONS CHOPPED FRESH PARSLEY OR CORIANDER

JUICE OF ½ LEMON

METHOD

Heat the oil in a large pan and cook the onion and garlic for 5 minutes until softened and golden. Stir in the rice and cook for a minute or two, turning to coat the grains in oil.

Stir in the stock, saffron and chilli flakes. Bring to the boil and simmer for 20 minutes or so, until the grains are tender.

Stir in the parsley or coriander, and lemon juice and serve.

ranch-style pit-baked beans

I served these here beans when I was down on the Benjamin Ranch in Kansas. Them cowboys sure did find 'em mighty fine! Burppp!

SERVES 8

250 G (9 OZ) DRIED WHITE BEANS, SUCH AS NAVY OR CANNELLINI
    BEANS, SOAKED OVERNIGHT

1 ONION, FINELY CHOPPED

100 G (4 OZ) CHORIZO SAUSAGE OR SMOKED BACON/HAM,
    ROUGHLY CHOPPED

3 TABLESPOONS DARK MUSCOVADO SUGAR

1 TABLESPOON SOY SAUCE

1 TEASPOON WORCESTERSHIRE SAUCE

1 TABLESPOON ENGLISH MUSTARD

METHOD

Place the beans in a large pan of fresh water, bring to the boil and boil hard for 10 minutes. Drain the beans and return to the pan.

Stir in the chopped onion, meat, sugar, soy, Worcestershire sauce and English mustard. Cover with water, bring back to the boil, and then cover and cook in a pre-heated oven (170°C/325°F/gas mark 3) for 1½–2 hours or until the beans are tender, adding extra water from time to time if necessary. You could cook your beans on top of the stove for the same amount of time, but remember to check the water levels every 15 minutes. Serve with grilled pork sausages or ribs.

peppy's jamaican rice and peas

This is a very traditional Caribbean side dish and it's also regarded as the Jamaican coat of arms. The peas are either red kidney beans, pigeon peas or black-eyed peas, not the standard green variety. Most are available at the supermarket or in a Caribbean food shop, either dried or in cans. My mum would cook this on most Sundays and all the children would be so impatient that half the pot was eaten before we sat down to eat. It's divinely delicious.

SERVES 8

1 ONION OR 3 SPRING ONIONS, FINELY CHOPPED

1 TABLESPOON SUNFLOWER OIL

25 G (1 OZ) BUTTER

2 GARLIC CLOVES, PEELED AND FINELY CHOPPED

1 RED FINGER CHILLI, SEEDED AND VERY FINELY CHOPPED

450 G (1 LB) LONG-GRAIN RICE

2 SPRIGS OF FRESH THYME

7.5 CM (3 IN) CINNAMON STICK (OPTIONAL)

400 G (14 OZ) TIN RED KIDNEY BEANS, BLACK-EYED PEAS OR
   PIGEON PEAS, DRAINED AND RINSED

125 G (4½ OZ) CREAMED COCONUT, COARSELY GRATED

1 LITRE (1¾ PINTS) HOT WATER

SALT AND FRESHLY GROUND BLACK PEPPER

METHOD

Fry the onion in the oil and butter for 2 minutes, then add the garlic and chilli and fry for another 2 minutes over a medium heat.

Stir in the rice, thyme and cinnamon stick (if using) until everything is well coated in the oil.

Pour in the kidney beans or peas, add the grated creamed coconut and stir until the coconut has dissolved so it's nice and creamy.

Then stir in the water with ½ teaspoon of salt, bring to the boil, cover and cook over a low heat for 25–30 minutes.

Remove from the heat and set aside, undisturbed, for 5 minutes.

Remove the thyme and cinnamon (if using), season to taste with salt and pepper and serve.

crazy crunchy crispy coleslaw

I go for a mayo-free coleslaw. It's particularly good with barbecued chicken burgers and potato dishes. Let those flavours mingle together for a few hours before serving the coleslaw. The result is a mouthwatering success.

SERVES 6

½ TEASPOON CUMIN SEEDS

1 SMALL WHITE CABBAGE, SHREDDED

1 SMALL RED ONION, THINLY SLICED

2 TART GREEN APPLES, CORED AND THINLY SLICED

2 RED JALAPENO CHILLIES

3 TABLESPOONS OLIVE OIL

1 TEASPOON WALNUT OIL (OPTIONAL)

JUICE OF 1 LIME

1 TEASPOON WHITE WINE VINEGAR

SALT AND FRESHLY GROUND BLACK PEPPER

METHOD

Place the cumin seeds in a small non-stick frying pan and cook over a medium heat for a couple of minutes, until they begin to offer up a delightful aroma and turn a little darker.

Place the cabbage, onion, apples, chillies, oils, lime juice, vinegar and cumin seeds in a large bowl and toss together well. Season to taste and chill until needed.

flamed polenta chips

These little golden flamed chips have a lovely texture and go brilliantly with your favourite salsas and dips. There are lots of ideas in the Basic Recipes section of this book if you're in need of some inspiration.

SERVES 6

1.2 LITRES (2 PINTS) BOILING WATER

½ TEASPOON SALT

200 G (7 OZ) INSTANT POLENTA

25 G (1 OZ) BUTTER

OLIVE OIL, FOR BRUSHING

METHOD

Place the water and salt in a large pan and return to the boil. Pour in the polenta, stirring constantly until smooth and thickened. Beat in the butter.

Pour the polenta on to an oiled baking sheet and spread out to a thickness of about 1 cm (½ in). Allow to cool completely.

Brush the surface of the polenta with a little more oil, then cut into fingers 1 cm (½ in) wide.

Cook in a heated chargrill pan for 2–3 minutes, turning until crisp and charred with lovely bar marks. Serve immediately with a salsa for dipping.

beefsteak mediterranean
tomatoes

Try to look out for large beefsteak tomatoes with lots of flavour. The 'marmande' variety from Provence, France and Morocco is absolutely superb and is occasionally available here during the summer months.

SERVES 6

6 FIRM BEEFSTEAK TOMATOES

4 TABLESPOONS OLIVE OIL

4 GARLIC CLOVES, PEELED AND FINELY CHOPPED

1 TABLESPOON CHOPPED FRESH OREGANO OR MARJORAM

SALT AND FRESHLY GROUND BLACK PEPPER

12 PITTED BLACK OLIVES, FINELY CHOPPED

METHOD

Cut the tomatoes in half and place rounded-side down in a shallow dish.

Sprinkle each one with some olive oil, garlic, oregano or marjoram, salt and pepper and set aside for 1 hour or until you are ready to cook them.

Sprinkle the tomatoes with the chopped olives and cook them in a hot oven or under a medium-hot grill for 10–12 minutes. Alternatively, lift them on to the side of the barbecue and cook, rounded-side down only, for about 10–12 minutes until tender.

fiery green beans, courgettes
and broccoli with lemon thyme

Colour is often so important when it comes to food, and this vegetable dish could quite easily take centre stage, it's so attractive.

SERVES 6

50 G (2 OZ) BUTTER

1 RED PIMIENTO, SEEDED AND SLICED

1 TEASPOON CHOPPED FRESH LEMON THYME

4 TABLESPOONS WATER

1 SMALL HEAD OF BROCCOLI, CUT INTO SMALL FLORETS

225 G (8 OZ) GREEN BEANS, TOPPED, TAILED AND CUT IN HALF

2 COURGETTES, CUT INTO BATONS 4 CM (1½ IN) LONG x ½ CM (¼ IN) WIDE

SALT AND FRESHLY GROUND BLACK PEPPER

METHOD

Heat half the butter in a frying pan, add the pimiento and thyme and cook for 3–4 minutes. Remove and set aside. Put the remaining butter and water in the frying pan and when it starts to bubble, add the broccoli and beans. Cover and cook for 3–4 minutes over a medium heat. The water should almost completely evaporate. Add the courgettes, the fried pimiento and thyme. Toss for another 2–3 minutes, season with salt and pepper and serve.

stir-fried udon noodles

Udon are thick, white Japanese-style noodles, but you can use any type of noodle you like for this dish – try regular Chinese-style egg noodles, or the fine rice noodles. Mirin is a sweet sake used for cooking – you can use a medium sherry if you can't get hold of it.

I love to serve this with any Oriental-style food, including both Thai and Chinese. Try it as an accompaniment to *Maple-glazed Duck with Plum and Cinnamon Dipping Sauce* (page 38), *Clare's Chinese Crispy Belly Pork* (page 60), or *Amazonian Monkfish Kebabs* (page 87).

SERVES 6

250 G (9 OZ) DRIED UDON NOODLES

1 TABLESPOON VEGETABLE OIL

1 TEASPOON SESAME OIL

3 CM (1¼ IN) PIECE FRESH ROOT GINGER, FINELY CHOPPED

2 GARLIC CLOVES, PEELED AND FINELY CHOPPED

1 RED CHILLI, SEEDED AND THINLY SLICED LENGTHWAYS

BUNCH OF SALAD ONIONS, SHREDDED

4 TABLESPOONS TOASTED SESAME SEEDS

2 TABLESPOONS SOY SAUCE

1 TABLESPOON MIRIN

A FEW DROPS OF RICE VINEGAR

METHOD

Cook the noodles in a large pan of boiling water according to the packet instructions. Cool by rinsing under cold water, then drain well.

Heat the oils in a wok and stir-fry the cooked noodles, ginger, garlic and chilli for 3–4 minutes until just beginning to brown. Stir in the salad onions and sesame seeds and stir-fry for 1 minute.

Stir in the soy sauce, mirin and a few drops of rice vinegar, to taste. Turn into a large bowl and serve immediately.

basic recipes

sweet mango salsa
Particularly good served with pork or duck.

SERVES 4

1 LARGE, RIPE MANGO, SKINNED, SEEDED
  AND FINELY DICED
12 RADISHES, FINELY DICED
JUICE OF 1 LIME
1 TABLESPOON OLIVE OIL
2 TABLESPOONS CHOPPED FRESH CORIANDER
A FEW SHAKES OF TABASCO
SALT AND FRESHLY GROUND BLACK PEPPER

Toss together the mango, radishes, lime juice, olive oil
and coriander. Add Tabasco, salt and pepper to taste,
then chill until ready to serve.

salsa verde
I like to serve this with all kinds of fish.

SERVES 4

2-4 GREEN CHILLIES
8 SPRING ONIONS
2 GARLIC CLOVES
50 G (2 OZ) SALTED CAPERS
1 SPRIG OF FRESH TARRAGON
1 BUNCH OF FRESH PARSLEY
JUICE AND GRATED ZEST OF 1 LIME
JUICE OF 1 LEMON
4 TABLESPOONS OLIVE OIL
1 TABLESPOON GREEN TABASCO
FRESHLY GROUND BLACK PEPPER

Halve the chillies and discard the seed. Trim the spring
onions and peel and halve the garlic cloves. Pulse briefly
in a food processor until roughly chopped. Using your
fingertips, wipe the excess salt off the capers, but don't
rinse them in water. Add the capers to the food
processor with the tarragon and parsley and pulse again
until fairly finely chopped.

Transfer to a small bowl and stir in the lime juice and
zest, lemon juice and olive oil. Stir the mixture loosely so
the citrus juice and oil do not emulsify. Add green
Tabasco and black pepper to taste.

Chill until ready to serve, but do not keep for more
than 8 hours.

mexican aztec tomato salsa
A classic salsa, particularly good with barbecued meat.

SERVES 6-8

6 TOMATOES, SKINNED, SEEDED AND DICED
1 MEDIUM RED ONION, FINELY CHOPPED
2 GARLIC CLOVES, PEELED AND CRUSHED
2 TABLESPOONS FRESHLY SQUEEZED LIME JUICE
2 GREEN CHILLIES, SEEDED AND VERY FINELY
  CHOPPED
4 TABLESPOONS CHOPPED FRESH CORIANDER
SALT AND FRESHLY GROUND BLACK PEPPER

Mix all the ingredients together, spoon into a bowl and
chill in the fridge for 1 hour.

chimichurri
This is a traditional Argentinian relish that is spooned
over barbecued meats and served with empanadas
(page 84).

SERVES 6

1 ONION, ROUGHLY CHOPPED
1 GREEN PEPPER, SEEDED AND ROUGHLY
  CHOPPED
1 TOMATO, ROUGHLY CHOPPED
2 TABLESPOONS FRESH PARSLEY LEAVES
2 GARLIC CLOVES, PEELED AND ROUGHLY
CHOPPED
5 TABLESPOONS WHITE WINE VINEGAR
2 TABLESPOONS OLIVE OIL
SALT AND FRESHLY GROUND BLACK PEPPER

Place the onion, green pepper, tomato, parsley and garlic in a liquidizer or food processor and whizz until finely chopped. Add the vinegar and oil, whizz again, then season to taste. Before serving, chill for an hour.

chilli jam

Always a winner and goes with absolutely anything.

SERVES 4

1-2 TABLESPOONS SUNFLOWER OIL

1 ONION, FINELY CHOPPED

2 GARLIC CLOVES, PEELED AND FINELY CHOPPED

2 RED CHILLIES, SEEDED AND FINELY CHOPPED

JUICE OF 1 ORANGE

1 TABLESPOON CLEAR HONEY

1 TABLESPOON MALT VINEGAR

2 TABLESPOONS TOMATO KETCHUP

Heat the oil in a small pan and cook the onion for 2–3 minutes. Add the garlic and chillies and cook for a further 2 minutes until softened. Stir in the orange juice, honey, vinegar and ketchup and simmer gently for 5 minutes. Serve warm or cold.

teasing taco sauce

This piquant sauce is delicious served with taco shells and beans.

SERVES 4

1 TABLESPOON SUNFLOWER OIL

1 SMALL ONION, FINELY CHOPPED

2 GARLIC CLOVES, PEELED AND FINELY CHOPPED

½ TEASPOON CUMIN SEEDS

1 STAR ANISE

2 TOMATOES, ROUGHLY CHOPPED

2 TABLESPOONS SOY SAUCE

2 TABLESPOONS CLEAR HONEY

2 TABLESPOONS WINE VINEGAR

1 TABLESPOON CHILLI SAUCE

½ TEASPOON SALT

Heat the oil in a small pan and cook the onion and garlic with the cumin and star anise for 3–4 minutes until softened. Add the tomatoes and cook for a further 3–4 minutes. Stir in the soy sauce, honey, vinegar, chilli sauce and salt. Bring to the boil and simmer rapidly for 5–10 minutes until thickened and pulpy. Serve warm or cold.

sweet chilli sauce

A refreshing accompaniment to almost any cooked meats and fish.

MAKES 175 ML (6 FL OZ)

150 G (5 OZ) CASTER SUGAR

300 ML (10 FL OZ) WATER

1 LIME

100 G (4 OZ) RED FINGER CHILLIES, SEEDED AND VERY FINELY CHOPPED

6 FRESH MINT LEAVES, FINELY CHOPPED

Put the sugar and water into a pan and leave over a low heat until the sugar has completely dissolved. Remove the zest of the lime with a potato peeler, taking care not to remove the bitter white pith from underneath. Cut the zest into very fine shreds, bunch them together and very finely chop. Squeeze out the juice from the lime.

Bring the mixture to the boil, add the lime zest and cook for about 3 minutes until the syrup lightly coats the back of a spoon. Add the chillies, remove from the heat and leave to cool before stirring in the mint.

sweet and sour apricot sauce

This rich and slightly tangy sauce is great with any kind of meat, especially pork.

MAKES 450 ML (15 FL OZ)

2 TABLESPOONS SUNFLOWER OIL

1 ONION, VERY FINELY CHOPPED

1 GARLIC CLOVE, PEELED AND CRUSHED

5 CM (2 IN) FRESH ROOT GINGER, PEELED
   AND FINELY GRATED

400 G (14 OZ) CAN APRICOTS IN NATURAL JUICE

3 TABLESPOONS LEMON JUICE

5 TABLESPOONS LIGHT SOFT BROWN SUGAR

3 TABLESPOONS DARK SOY SAUCE

75 ML (3 FL OZ) WHITE WINE VINEGAR

2 TABLESPOONS TOMATO PURÉE

SALT AND FRESHLY GROUND BLACK PEPPER

Heat the oil in a medium-sized pan. Add the onion and fry for 5 minutes until soft and very lightly browned. Add the garlic and the ginger to the pan and fry for 1 minute.

Drain the canned apricots, reserving the juice. Put the apricots, 2 tablespoons of the apricot juice and the lemon juice into a food processor and blend until smooth.

Add the apricot purée to the onions with the rest of the ingredients and leave to simmer for 25–30 minutes until reduced and thickened. Serve hot or cold.

chiang-mai thai dipping sauce

Ideal for serving with plainly cooked meat and fish.

MAKES 150 ML (5 FL OZ)

6 TABLESPOONS RICE OR WHITE WINE VINEGAR

4 TABLESPOONS CASTER SUGAR

½ TEASPOON SALT

1 CLOVE GARLIC, PEELED AND FINELY CHOPPED

2 RED BIRDSEYE CHILLIES, THINLY SLICED

1 TEASPOON CHOPPED FRESH CORIANDER

1 SPRING ONION, TRIMMED AND THINLY SLICED

Mix together the vinegar and the sugar until the sugar has completely dissolved. Now stir in the remaining ingredients and serve in little bowls as a dipping sauce or drizzled over simply grilled meats and fish.

mellow minty yoghurt sauce

A classic accompaniment to any Indian or Middle Eastern meat dishes.

SERVES 4

175 G (6 OZ) GREEK OR WHOLEMILK NATURAL
   YOGHURT

3 TABLESPOONS CHOPPED FRESH MINT

1 TEASPOON MINT JELLY, WARMED

SALT AND FRESHLY GROUND BLACK PEPPER

Simply mix all the ingredients together and chill for at least 1 hour before serving.

best ever mustard french dressing

This is really useful for tossing through salad leaves, stirring into hot potatoes and adding extra flavour to other salad-like side dishes.

SERVES 8

2 TABLESPOONS WHITE WINE VINEGAR

2 TABLESPOONS DIJON MUSTARD

8 TABLESPOONS OLIVE OIL

SALT AND FRESHLY GROUND BLACK PEPPER

Mix the vinegar and mustard together and whisk in the oil until thick and creamy. Season and chill until required.

index